# Quit Losing Talent:

# Expanded Edition

*Twenty Leadership Tactics to Win, Keep, & Inspire Great Employees*

Mike Harbour

"Train people well enough so they can leave,
treat them well enough so they don't want to."

—Sir Richard Branson[1]

# Table of Contents

# Praise For *Quit Losing Talent, Expanded Edition*

"With *Quit Losing Talent*, Mike Harbour has created the modern playbook for talent management. Mike's deep experience as a leadership coach shines through in his practical and action-oriented tactics."

Mark Amox, CEO of Unity Health Hospital System

"This expanded edition is a must read for all leaders who are passionate about refining their leadership skills. This book sets up a leader for success."

Hope Caraway, Executive Director of HR at White River Health

"As CEO of Ochsner Baptist, I see how the tactics taught in *Quit Losing Talent* can help teams create a space for open dialogue, collaboration, and the kind of trust so fundamental to winning and keeping employees."

Beth Walker, CEO of Ochsner Baptist

"Quit Losing Talent is a Must Have for organizations looking to enhance their culture, reduce turnover and increase communication with their team. Mike's QLT program has our leaders asking for more as they continue to find value in the training and resources. Utilizing the QLT program has helped us build leadership confidence, hire right, and reduce turnover. I highly recommended the QLT program to leaders in all industries!"

Tiffany Johnson, Director of Resource Development at Infinity Health

"*Quit Losing Talent* is a superb resource, packed with wisdom and knowledge that will undoubtedly enhance anyone's understanding of effective talent management. *Quit Losing Talent* is a powerhouse of valuable insights and practical guidance. I am confident this book will be an indispensable reference for professionals at every stage of their talent management journey."

Mickey Trent, Healthcare Executive Recruiter

"Here are the top two reasons you will want to share this book with your team. First, it covers what is, and will continue to be, one of the most pressing challenges facing your organization. Second, it is written by one of the nation's leading authorities on how to attract and retain the best people. The book is filled with practical wisdom and useful exercises, beginning with one of the best explanations I've seen of the why and how of integrating core values into your talent acquisition and retention process."

Joe Tye, coauthor of *Building a Culture of Ownership in Healthcare*


"Mike, your experience and insight are both powerful and objective. Employees are our most valuable assets. Well-functioning teams not only produce exceptional results, but continuously strive to exceed expectations. I would encourage any leader or organization that wants to improve retention and improve outcomes to apply the principles outlined in *Quit Losing Talent*."

Mary Dunn, Healthcare Executive Search Consultant


"*Quit Losing Talent* offers practical insights and actionable ideas to help any team develop staff in a way that makes the whole organization flourish. Every organization I encounter would benefit from implementing these strategies, and any manager can make a difference armed with ideas from this book."

Jeane Hendrix, Registered Nurse


## Praise for *Quit Losing Talent, First Edition*

"This little book is packed with helpful nuggets. I find big changes often start with small shifts in how we think about things. Mike Harbour is a master at getting the reader to evaluate what may be long-held assumptions around what attracts and retains great people. *Quit Losing Talent* has a timely, even urgent, message for the many companies struggling in the post-pandemic era."

Quint Studer, author of *The Busy Leader's Handbook*

"*Quit Losing Talent* is incredibly practical and tactical. A combination that is not easy to create but one that reflects a high degree of respect for the reader who has extraordinary demands on their time. "

Dr. Diana Hendal, PharmD, former hospital CEO, author of *Responsible*, and *Trauma to Triumph*

"Mike Harbour worked with our supervisory staff over the course of a year to prepare for an agency transition. Utilizing his leadership strategies and guidance, the supervisors developed as effective team leaders and team builders with productive employees who love what they do! *Quit Losing Talent* outlines many of the things Mike helped us implement in our company."

Sharon Murphy, RN, ACRN, CEO Emeritus McGregor Clinic

"Keeping and attracting inspired team members has never been as challenging as it is in today's environment. Yet in this book by leadership and employee retention expert, Mike Harbour, Mike provides us with the keys to understanding and transforming our approach to ensuring a 'stellar' workforce."

Brian Cunningham, Healthcare Leader and Author of *The Leadership Revolution* and *Our AQ (Awareness Quotient)*.

# Foreword

When I left active-duty Army service at the end of 1998, I took a couple of months off and then began working for a company called Management Recruiters International. I was looking for a management job in healthcare, but this company hired me to help build a healthcare recruiting division.

In January of 1999, I began talking to, recruiting, and interviewing healthcare leaders from the C-Suite down to the director level of hospitals and healthcare-related companies. Since then, I have personally interviewed over 20,000 leaders learning about them, their leadership style, and dreams and goals for taking teams to the next level.

I have helped companies recruit, hire, and lead people in hundreds of organizations. I have helped them improve the recruitment process and retention of new and tenured employees. I don't like to call myself an expert, but it is through extensive experience that I have learned some of the best practices to serve you better.

There is no greater calling than serving others by helping them be better leaders and keep the people they lead. It took me a while to realize this is what I was called to do, but I believe my mission is to help everyone be a more effective leader and help every employee be led well, because it's what everyone deserves, including you.

I have led hundreds of people, coached hundreds more who weren't my employees, and advised executives and their teams to implement the framework and tools in our system to success.

If you have the desire to create a culture where talent is attracted to you, stays with you, and performs at a high level for you — the ideas and tools in this book are for you.

# The Quit Losing Talent (QLT) Framework

The Quit Losing Talent (QLT) Framework has four main strategies—one for each of the phases of your employee talent lifecycle. Strengthening your company's Attraction, Activation, Retention, and Release strategies will create a framework for talent retention. Each strategy is critical to running a profitable, efficient organization with the kind of flourishing culture that draws high performers to your vision. Like a truck running on four tires, having a poor strategy in any of the four areas will create a talent drain from your organization. Companies struggling to draw and keep talent may be running low on all four tires—all four strategies need attention.

## Practice *Sapere Vedere*

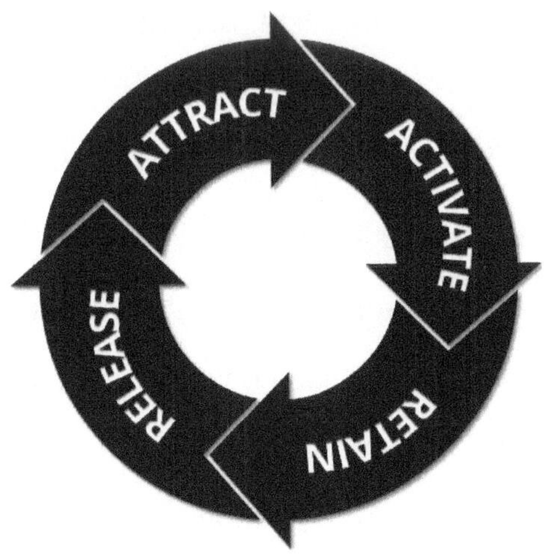


## BE The Leader Who Makes the Culture Stick

**Attraction** involves recruiting and becoming an employer of choice

**Activation** begins with onboarding and leads to mastery

**Retention** strengthens engagement and unlocks and growth

**Release** includes the exit process, offboarding, learning from losses

Over time, your effectiveness with each strategy will naturally shift. Increased pressures in the marketplace or changes in the talent pool can increase your company's need to improve performance with one or more strategies. Once your QLT Framework is in place, each of the four strategies will provide structure for nurturing talent throughout the lifetime of your employees. But like any strategy, it only works when implemented. Stay engaged as the leader to reward and motivate implementations of proven tactics to lock talent into your organization.

## Quit Losing Talent Culture

Something powerful happens when a company implements the QLT Framework: the company culture begins to shift. Any company that builds a Quit Losing Talent Culture becomes a place where talented individuals from our community and industry are drawn to work. Evidence of a culture shift begins to show up as you work on strengthening your team's attraction, activation, retention, and release strategies.

## You know you have a QLT Culture when:

Talent and effort are recognized daily.

New hires are equipped and launched systematically.

Vision for the future is clear and communicated regularly.

When talent leaves, they leave us as better people and employees.

Leaders and employees are developed to their fullest potential.

# Sapere Vedere

Leadership is not for the faint of heart. Whether you're commanding a multinational corporation, or putting out fires from your lonely desk on the frontlines of customer care, the world of work demands you step up to lead.

Many of the problems facing us at work are not new. One in particular has been on the horizon for decades: the talent crisis. In every industry, reality has forced leaders to admit we need to invest in our workers so that our companies can thrive. In the beginning, it felt like a victory to hear resounding agreement about what our companies needed to thrive in the long term. But after several decades dancing with the obvious answer, it's clear that most of our organizations have only given this solution lip service.

Developing people is never convenient.

There is always some emergency, some urgent priority, some flashy opportunity that seems more pressing than the work of long-term talent development. Many leaders believe they will get to it but never develop the kind of universal training pathway, or individual development plans that flesh out their good intentions. They imagine that the small, occasional investments in employee well-being will get the ball rolling. But often, these investments are not strategic. They lack impact because they don't flow from one of the primary practices of leadership – something I teach as the intentional practice of *sapere vedere*.[3]

Leonardo da Vinci popularized the phrase *sapere vedere*, using it to mean visual literacy—educating your eye to understand and unpack what it is seeing. Translated into English, the phrase means "learning how to see."[4] The practice of learning how to see in life and business is critical to helping your team and your company flourish. Simply surviving the ups and downs of your industry doesn't mean you are truly seeing what you need to see.

---

**"When we change the way we look at things, things we look at begin to change."**

—Wayne Dyer[5]

---

Just as millions of tourists walk through the Louvre every year[6] without fully appreciating what they see, so many of us push through the demands of our daily work without really grasping what happens. Top leaders and successful managers in every industry rise above the masses to practice *sapere vedere* at work, drawing insights and clarity from the past and applying it strategically in the present in order to envision and capture a better future.

First time managers and veteran leaders alike need to learn how to see through three lenses: hindsight, foresight, insight.

# Hindsight

It can be painful to look closely at the past. The more tired, overworked, and pressured we become, the less being retrospective sounds like a good idea. But desperate times force us to look at the uncomfortable realities in our workplaces.

That's what happened to Melanie Wallace. After losing 20% of her staff every month over a brutal 18 months, she was forced to reduce admissions to her skilled nursing facility due to unstable staffing. She used agency staffing to protect against unsafe care ratios. But the same agency nurses designed to stabilize the employee loss increased turnover as long-term employees resented the higher wages paid to (and lower performance provided by) agency staff. By the time her team made three ghost hires within a 90-day period, Melanie was desperate enough to take a hard look at the organization's hiring and onboarding paradigm.[8]

Great companies learn how to routinely look to the past, and evaluate successes and failures in the practice of hindsight. Hindsight can reveal unsatisfactory patterns and disprove accepted wisdom. Truisms and long-standing assumptions unseated by hindsight include things like:

| Assumption | Reality |
| --- | --- |
| "We're paying them, they'll do whatever we say they have to do." | Management by paycheck is failing, and worker shortages mean that pay no longer equals effort or compliance. |
| "Employee satisfaction doesn't matter as much as customer satisfaction." | Customer service will reflect employee satisfaction; employees are the primary driver of customer experience and complaint resolution. |

| "If we're not willing to give raises, there's nothing we can do to make employees happier." | We're so used to throwing money at problems that we can start to think all problems are money problems. Most employees don't leave for financial reasons; they leave because they're miserable in our culture. Make efforts to help employees feel valued, provide growth opportunities, and reduce sources of friction in the environment. Morale will respond. |
|---|---|
| "Remote work isn't even an option for our industry." | When remote work isn't an option, explore ways to be flexible with schedules and don't rely on "this is the way we have always done it." Remember how many industries did "the impossible" during the COVID pandemic. It turns out more things are "options" if we're willing to think outside the box. |
| "Pair new hires with our most seasoned people and they will learn how to work." | Simply watching a high performer do their work at top speed rarely equips a trainee. Leadership, mentorship, and talent development are skills completely distinct from the skills of many roles. Pairing a new hire with a skilled technician or busy team member can be a disaster if they don't have a framework for transferring skills, giving feedback, and equipping the new hire. It also may be necessary to offset the experienced team member's workload so there is room to teach the new hire as they go. |
| "People just don't want to work today." | Burnout can spark pessimism about the entire group of people we find ourselves leading. Whether it's an age group, or type of worker we have become disillusioned with, our negative perceptions can change the way we see the people we're leading. We get what we expect, measure, and hold people accountable for. We also have a profound impact on the motivation levels and energy our people bring to work. Learn to draw and reinforce the energy of those we lead, and fight the bias that burnout can cast. |

One thing hindsight teaches every leader in our time is that we cannot keep delaying employee development and engagement. Employee engagement has made minimal if any significant improvement in the last 20 years. Seeing problems coming does nothing to help us if we don't take action. If a team is hurting in the talent performance area, it likely means talent development strategies have been inadequate for some time.

Perhaps it sounds basic to say, "if we don't like what we have, we have to change what we're doing." But a lot of what is thwarting your success are problems in the foundation. Experts and successful companies alike agree that we will have to improve our talent development strategies if we want staffing quality to rise. Haphazard feedback and financial incentives will not move the needle. In hindsight, we must become aware that a workshop once a year, or even once per quarter, is like throwing our people in the microwave and warming them up, but not infusing them with learning.

Whether you're a CEO or a solopreneur or a frontline worker with no direct reports, what would happen if you examined the past for some hindsight? Grab a thinking partner, a clear headspace, and ask yourself some honest, simple questions about what's working and what isn't.

Maybe take a minute now, and use it to reflect on patterns. You'll take them with you into the next piece of *sapere vedere* once you've got them in view. Here are some reflection questions to get you started:

## Sharpen Your Hindsight:

- What are my/our team's main vulnerabilities, and are they new? What have my/our historical weaknesses been?

- What are my/our team's major sources of frustration, chaos, and unplanned changes? What are the causes of these? Are they new or recurring? Getting worse or better?

- What activities, products, teams, or priorities have been the greatest consumers of energy/resources/time? What has the value of these been, and how is the return on time investment (ROTI)? What is lacking that would improve the return? When they've performed the best (and worst), what have seemed to be the causes?

- Looking back, where did I plan to be now? Have things changed? Am I making no progress, slow progress, intermittent progress, or negative progress?

If answering these questions is time consuming, difficult, or anxiety-producing, don't judge yourself too harshly. This kind of leadership activity gets easier and quicker with practice. Even stumbling through it a few times will prepare you to grow meaningful, weighty insights from ongoing reflection.

Partner up with a coach or colleague to energize this process. But if you have to do it alone, be encouraged; this is the good kind of hard work. If you don't like what you learn, knowing where you have been is an important step in creating lasting change. It's not enough to say we must change; knowing what we are changing can free us from cycles of repeated mistakes.

As you process the past and strengthen your skills in hindsight, remember that you don't have to stay stuck. The next piece of *sapere vedere* builds a bridge to the future you're working to create.

# Foresight

When we start thinking about building success for our careers, or our companies and the people we lead, we usually think about what success itself looks like. We build a visionary picture of what future success entails. To bring it into focus, we imagine how things are going, who we are helping, what is being created, what is our profit, and what resources we are leveraging. This paints a kind of "finish line" picture of flourishing in our work.

But if we're not careful, those pictures of future success can be little more than fantasies. That's where foresight comes in. Foresight asks who we need to BE—who that future demands we BEcome. What characteristics, values, practices, and competencies do we need to develop in order to produce that kind of success? Foresight is looking into the future and asking not just where we want to go, but working to wisely discern who we will need to BEcome on the way there.

Achieving success is not the goal, BEcoming the leader who can achieve success and then sustain the progress is the goal.

It's a bit like the way performance psychologists teach their clients to activate success through visualization. They do so not by having them daydream about the moment of success and achievement in isolation, but rather by training them to visualize themselves completing the behaviors that drive success.

If you want to successfully complete an ultramarathon, don't just visualize crossing the finish line; visualize the alarm going off while it's still dark, smiling to yourself as you lace trainers on your sleepy feet and head out into the drizzling morning to get your daily training run in. Visualize hitting mile twenty, feeling a blister forming, and smiling to yourself even as sunblock drips in your eye, confident that you're the kind of person who pushes through and has victory in spite of difficulty.

Foresight isn't a fantasy; it's an honest discovery of the person your dreams demand you become in order to arrive at success. It's a way of taking ownership of the journey, not shopping for lightning bolts of success. Instead of waiting for great employees to show up and manage themselves, what would happen if you became the kind of leader who could challenge and inspire employees to become great, learn to lead themselves, and deliver excellence to the team every day?

Even if the only person you are leading is yourself, practicing foresight to discover who you need to become is a leadership activity. The practice of foresight acknowledges that our values, character, and cultivated practices exert massive influence on what happens in our lives.

Because of this, foresight emphasizes values and character much more than results and accomplishments. The moments of achievement flow from the virtue and habits that have developed at the center of who we have become through daily effort and honest reflection. It's our values and character that we need to cultivate with the long term in mind.

Do the habits we have create success for us? Most of us have some habits that serve us, and others that don't. When you're working on hindsight it's worth taking a good look at your habits to discover what habits might be holding you back. But when it comes time for foresight, part of charting a path into the future is understanding what habits and practices would support you on your way.

One of the reasons I push this discipline of asking what habits and practices support us in becoming the person our vision demands is because it gives us a reality check. It's way too easy to give lip service to a list of values on the wall and pretend we've "built our business on them." Actually building according to our values requires a clear picture of what actions, processes, behaviors, and habits those values translate into.

Who do you need to become to get where you want to go? What does it look like to do today's work on the path to that future? Take a few minutes right now and use foresight to define your values. List examples of clear behaviors and actions that embody and perpetuate those values. Ask yourself what kinds of actions are needed immediately, in the next six months, and five years from now.

# Foresight & Team Culture

In working with hundreds—if not thousands—of leaders, I often hear, "when I get into a leadership role, I will lead differently." I too said this early in my professional life. Yet many repeat the same unsuccessful leadership style and mistakes that created many of the problems and challenges their boss faced.

If you want to be a different leader, you need to define those differences. What will your style look and feel like to those you lead? What will they experience that is different from past leadership?

Doing this paints a unique picture of the future, of you in the future, and of the rhythm of your success in motion. We probe and strengthen our foresight before moving to insight because we want the clarity of our goals to influence our search for insight.

BEcoming is a process of growth, adaptation, and change. You don't arrive at leadership; it's a process of BEcoming. What are you BEcoming? Who are you BEcoming?

Culture on the other hand is created by the behaviors that express and bring our values to life. The values must be defined, modeled, and lived out daily. What culture do you want to drive in your leadership? The team creates the culture, but the leader drives it through leading, communicating clarity, and course correcting when someone loses focus.

You must look into the future using foresight questions and then work backward from that future destination using insight. If you skip this, the culture will be created by the loudest voices on the team, good or bad.

The Big Hairy Audacious Goal (BHAG) question I challenge leaders to ask themselves is, "twelve months from now, what do I want the culture and success of my team to look, feel, and be like?" Once you answer this question, revisit it quarterly to evaluate your progress and keep moving in that direction.

Now that we've sharpened our perception toward the future, let's bring it all together by shifting to the third practice of *sapere vedere*: insight.

# Insight

It's not enough to simply stare into the rearview mirror, or get caught up dreaming about greener pastures, without action. Analyzing old patterns isn't enough if you don't figure out what to do with that knowledge. Applied knowledge is insight. When refined through action that insight turns into wisdom.

What did your hindsight reflection show you? If you didn't take time yet to ask what the past is telling you, it's not too late; do it now. Then you'll be free to ask yourself what that information really means.

Sometimes patterns are superficial. Maybe your team has hired six new developers in the past year. The first three were over the age of 40, and the second three were under the age of 30. If the first three performed better, gaining mastery faster than the second three, all of whom have problems with consistency and accuracy in their performance, you might initially determine that your company should only hire applicants over the age of 40.

But insight would nudge you to look for other patterns. Ask what else besides age was different between the two groups. You might realize that the first three developers were hired to join a team of colleagues around their age, and during a time when the mentoring program was an in-person process. The three lower-performing team members all came on after the team went remote. In the chaos, mentoring opportunities were erratic at best. With the age difference, lack of camaraderie among new and old team members increased the sense of separation, yielding a poor transfer of knowledge and mastery from the existing staff to the new arrivals.

Insight says it's time to reimagine your mentoring program to meet the demands of virtual work. Insight says it's time to figure out how to strengthen your culture and connectedness, because that's one of the ways knowledge and mastery circulates through the team to develop strong, consistent talent.

To gain these kinds of insights, break down the silos of your comparison. In our developer performance example, this meant getting beyond the snapshot of the employee's demographics and performance and noticing trends in training and mentoring processes.

If you are an upper-level manager or executive leader, this means looking at things through an even larger lens, and sometimes comparing what is happening in your organization with the other companies in your space. Take for example, the companies who analyzed their company's financial returns and compared the trends with workforce resilience scores. According to a formal analysis done by Jeannotte, Hutchinson, and Kellerman, these results were quantified:

> Companies whose workforce had the highest average resilience scores demonstrated 42% higher return on assets and 3.7% higher annual return on equity. In addition, they showed 3.2x higher year-over-year growth… Employees who report to resilient leaders are themselves nearly three times as resilient as others. They're also 50% less burned out than employees whose leaders are not resilient. Teams with resilient leaders were 30% more productive. These teams were more innovative and more cognitively agile, too.[11]

Do you see that high level insight gathering? If you're going to prioritize your resources, focus, and risk investments in the team or company you are leading, you have to be able to draw some connections between key outcomes and the teams that produce them. None of this will happen if you don't make the space to step back and analyze.

## Insight on Your Habits + Process

One key area I want to highlight as a prime target for your *sapere vedere* practice is your own habits and processes. Too often, we blame the negative outcomes we experience on environmental factors. We think things "going wrong" or shifts in the world outside our control are responsible for things that don't go as planned.

But what if you're consistently getting those unplanned results? Chances are you're not just experiencing random bad luck. At least some things go consistently or cyclically wrong. Even if these forces and negative trends are completely out of your control, developing habits and processes to address and diffuse these negative forces can shift your results in an ongoing way.

Another way to say this is to say Insight doesn't just look for one-time actions to "fix" acute problems; Insight looks for the patterns under the problems and goes to work establishing new patterns.

As you read the chapters in this book, you'll notice talent lock techniques like the "S.T.A.Y. Development Process" that demonstrate the way successful companies continually feed their insights back into the team culture to help their people grow. No matter how grand the gesture, or epic the intervention, no one-off activity will have as great an impact as a successful process. So while you're looking for insights, don't skimp on evaluating your processes.

## Examples of Insights:

- A leader who is constantly overworking because they don't have people they can trust to hand important tasks and decisions off to. A quick fix would be making time to do a day or two of training for the one worst task they need to delegate. Insight goes beyond this to discover that this leader needs to develop a habit and process for mentoring and developing the capabilities of their team members in general so that they have more trusted, capable hands to collaborate with.

- A manager who always has to be on call because the staff doesn't have a problem-solving process or effective contingency decision tree to follow, needs to discover processes that can eliminate the need for their input by supporting the team when they're out of office.

- A worker who has a clear pathway for advancement, but keeps failing to set aside time to progress consistently may need an accountability process or task management habit that would keep next steps top of mind at the right time.

You may already know what processes and habits are needed for you to get where you're trying to go. Good for you; bring it into focus and ask yourself, "what would help me effectively build these things into my life? What else would I add to my strategy to take it to the next level?"

But if you don't know what habits or processes would support your success it may be time to ask around or do some research to figure out best practices from others. Experimenting is one of the best ways to fast track your progress and reduce unnecessary effort as you're on the pathway to your chosen future. If you build on the experiments of others (sometimes called "guided learning") you save even more time and effort.

Invite others into your thinking as partners, look for mentors or a coach to help you think outside the box and see new ideas. Even small improvements or a single useful insight can exponentially improve your results, especially as it is amplified over time.

## We All Have Biases

Insight requires perspective. Your own perspective is powerful and valuable, but wise leaders recognize that gaining multiple perspectives is a huge win for insight. Who has a different, but engaged, perspective on the success of your team? Any team hierarchy performs like the rungs of a ladder or the peaks of a mountain range. Every view has value for solving some question. Reach out to others who can add to your insights. And don't only look "above" you in the pecking order. Reach out above you, below you, and across the aisle from you to gain surprising insights through the perspectives of others. Every seat has its own insight advantage.

When looking around for perspectives to add to your insight, you may be wary of the biases of others. This is good; it can seem easier to find the biases of others. Maybe the operations director is going to care the most about utilization management, and the sales rep is going to care about customer complaints. Maybe the director will only care what it costs, and the new employee is distracted by how things worked at their previous workplace. The insights they can offer under these biases add great dimension to your own analysis. Let them be biased, and learn from them anyway!

Bias in some sense is only lethal if we silo according to that bias. Instead, gather the many voices together and gain perspective. When it comes time for any of us to practice insight, we've got to realize it isn't just others who are biased. We are too. It's natural for us to minimize our sense of bias, and give ourselves credit for thinking holistically. This is one of the reasons I interview leaders on The Lead Up Podcast. I gain great insight to do things differently than I have done them in the past. Every voice increases potential new ways to innovate or think differently in the future.

No one can think holistically alone. We need to learn to listen to others and allow their thinking to challenge our blind spots. We can never truly eliminate our biases, but by identifying them and broadening our perspective with input from others, we can be stronger for it. Where a single bias creates blind spots, a broad range of biases investigated together brings depth.

At the end of the day, insight comes from grabbing the evaluated experience from hindsight, and the dream for the future from foresight, and turning them into clarity about what actions will move us forward.

Without wonder and insight, leadership is just a trade or position; with wonder and insight, leadership becomes creation.

# How to Use This Book

Turnover dynamics will always be a linchpin of excellence on any team. Employee knowledge, skill, and shared culture are the largest assets your organization has to leverage. Your people are your competitive advantage. With worker mobility and talent shortages on a sharp upward trajectory, the teams that thrive, the brands that dominate, and the organizations that deliver strong returns do so by mastering the talent life cycle.

In our work at Harbour Resources and in my decades of helping companies excel in human resource operations, I've been amazed to see the resilience and innovation that good teams can manage even in the harshest of circumstances. Spikes in turnover and trends of increase in worker mobility are certainly harsh circumstances for many of us. Experience has convinced me that these pressures are perennial. To thrive in business today, our companies and teams need to become resilient, learning organizations.

As you flip through these pages you will discover a playbook of how to optimize and elevate your success in the four-part talent life cycle already at work in your company. This life cycle starts with attracting talent, and builds on it by activating, retaining, and even releasing that talent when an employee tenure ends.

# Talent Life Cycle

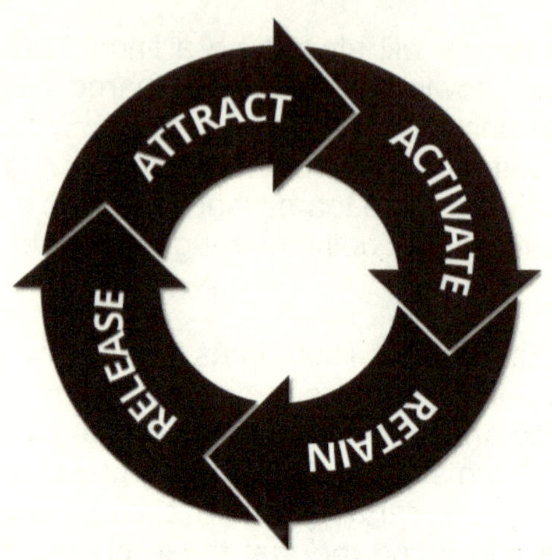


1.  **Attraction:** Magnetizing top talent out of the hiring pool and choosing new team members well.

2.  **Activation:** Robust onboarding and developing of new team members to achieve, produce, and engage with mastery at work.

3.  **Retention:** Keeping our best employees by dealing with barriers to engagement and developing increasing value in established team members.

4.  **Release:** Offboarding well and learning from employees who leave the company so the team is strengthened through turnover, and unhealthy turnover is eliminated.

I have organized this playbook in the order I often teach it to teams. We start with retaining the employees you currently have and then improve the offboarding and release process. We do that first before turning our attention to attracting new talent. We'll wrap up the book with the activation process. I want to leave you with a clear picture of what it looks like to turn an employee's talent on full blast, and set the tone for their best contribution to your company whether they are with you for a year or a decade.

If you have an urgent need to see improvement at some point in the talent life cycle, by all means, jump to the chapter that focuses on that. If you're about to post a new job ad, grab some shortcuts and insights from the attraction section. But if you're like most of us, all aspects of your organization's talent management could use improvement. Join me for an overview of what it looks like to make your company grow richer and stronger with each person who passes through your doors.

If we're going to lead our companies to success in the modern, mobilized, and globalized economy, we as leaders need to be brutally honest with ourselves about how company culture, employee development, and hiring practices are impacting our productivity and profit. Getting a clear snapshot of the human resource paradigm reveals a circular process of acquiring, developing, and engaging our talent.

If you want to quit losing talent (and who doesn't?!), you can eliminate problems and strengthen performance across all four phases of the employee lifecycle at your company. Each phase of an employee's tenure with you brings unique challenges and offers opportunities for increasing their value as part of the team.

Those four phases are Attraction, Activation, Retention, and Release.

Using talent lock strategies in each phase of your talent life cycle will develop momentum as it is implemented and mastered over time.

A company with a Quit Losing Talent (QLT) culture maximizes growth and problem solving at each stage of an employee's tenure. They'll draw out the best in potential hires, thoroughly onboard with skill and clarity, develop and ignite the performance of long-term employees, and even strengthen the team through strategic offboarding processes.

More often than not though, companies aren't doing a great job in at least two strategies, and may overlook one of the strategies entirely.

For the sake of this book, we'll start with Retention. Let's access the latent talent, and solidify the staying power of the team you already have. To do that we'll look at some key practices for keeping the strong performers and the raw talent already within your organization. These retention strategies are particularly aimed at eliminating the worst kind of turnover any business has: losing strong employees.

Next, we'll look at the final strategy related to any employee: Release. In my workshops, we often start with this crucial phase because losing an employee provides a valuable opportunity to mine the situation for insights. Don't just hold on, and wait for employees to "get out of the way." Offboarding with intentional release strategies paves the way for a new hire to have greater success than the person you're losing.

QLT tactics for releasing employees include activities that provide an onramp for excellent onboarding and future employee success. They may even make it possible to turn the employee who is about to leave into the new hire you need most.

Third we'll go to Attraction, helping you retire some tired techniques that simply don't bring the successful new hires you need. We'll replace them with some proven tactics for establishing a compelling employment brand, and sifting through the noisy hiring market to find high achievers for your team. This helps you hire with greater confidence, and even seeds your prospective talent pool by making you an employer of choice because of the reputation you develop.

And last we'll look at the Activation techniques that go beyond orientation to create mastery. These techniques are designed to reduce your turnover rate dramatically over time. Many of the poor performers and unmotivated employees on your team became this way because of things that happened (or didn't happen) during their first 90 days at your company! How someone starts, what they learn, and how they are equipped when they first enter your organization leaves a lasting imprint on their work behaviors for their entire time with you.

There are a lot of places to improve your organization's talent quotient. Even small improvements in each phase can stop the bleeding and shift your momentum in the right direction.

# Retention: Create a Talent Lock Culture

"Start the retention process when your employees are still open to staying, not after they've already told you they're leaving."

— Jeff Weiner[12]

It costs more to lose and replace our best talent than it does to take action that keeps them. Many studies tell us it costs one and a half to ten times an employee's salary to replace them. So, before we treat the vacancies on our team as talent attraction problems, let's tackle the most lucrative strategy in the entire talent lock toolkit: retention.

High performers are the most neglected part of many teams. We fail to coach them because we think they don't need us. We overwork them until they burn out.

Maybe your team is filled with the ghosts of high performers; they're burnt out, phoning it in, or barely keeping their heads above water. Burnout is not a sign of a low performer. It's your best talent taking the brunt of overwork and poor processes, and often carrying low-performing teammates. If you keep the focus on getting "better employees" instead of reversing the drivers of burnout, your hunt for talent will never end.

Retention tactics will reverse performance declines in your team members who are disengaged. I've been saying for years, "the world is screaming for leadership." The recent challenges in the workforce confirm this more than ever. The top reason an employee chooses to stay with us today is feeling that their leader cares about their development, and sees value in the work they offer each day. Without that, we lose the vitality, and eventually the presence, of our employees. This drives the deadliest turnover rate and will be avoided if we engage in talent retention tactics.

If you are feeling the squeeze of understaffing, you may be tempted to jump to the section that helps with attracting new employees. If you do that, you'll find techniques for making better hiring decisions, and attracting higher caliber prospects. But I want to challenge you first to recognize that the highest return on your investment for improving the talent equation at your organization comes from engaging the employees you already have.

We begin with some strategic strengthening of your current team for three reasons:

1.  It is less expensive to strengthen an existing employee's engagement than to replace them when they leave. The average cost to replace an employee is at least one and a half to ten times their annual earnings.

2.  Current employees impact the quality of new talent you attract. Leading them well creates a culture that makes talent want to stay with your organization. When they do this, they can help reduce errors in new employee selection, and fast track the excellent onboarding of new hires.

3.  Any improvements made to the culture before adding new employees will reduce the transferring of bad habits and expectations onto fresh additions to the team. If we don't do that, it won't matter how great the new employees we find are; they can't push upstream against the culture you're bringing them into.

As I write this book, I think back to my thirty years of experience in leadership. I can remember discussions about preparing for the worker shortages, baby boomer retirements, and plans to offset these coming challenges. Yet here we are reactively working to solve these problems in the here and now.

We can blame the COVID-19 pandemic, but really the pandemic only accelerated the challenges. It didn't cause them. We can blame the government, but that won't help us. The problems are ours to solve. Let's accept the challenge, and do the things others talk about doing.

Let's get started.

# Retention Tactic #1:
## *Target Check Your Values*

Imagine you've taken your team out for some unconventional team building. Instead of a trust fall, or skydiving together, you head to one of the trendy ax throwing barns near your office.

It is surprisingly hard to stick an ax in the center of a target twelve feet away. A few talented (or lucky) team members might stick their ax in the softer targets, but the harder the target (wood is tougher than cardboard), the more difficult it is to make it stick.

Like any game of targets, everyone can clearly see whether the ax landed or not and how close to the center each attempt landed. The target provides clarity for estimating and analyzing performance.

That's the beauty and painful truth about a bold target; it tells you where you are in relation to the goal.

At your company, you have lots of targets you're working to hit every day. Metrics, objectives, and benchmarks are all important, but one key target in any high-performing company is embodied in the company values.

Truitt Cathy, founder of Chick-fil-A was quoted as saying to his executives in a meeting, "Instead of us focusing on getting bigger, let's focus on getting better." He was challenging his leadership team to be values-driven, not profit- or size-driven. Values are the guiding lights of our actions, and the glue that holds the team together when it gets hard.

Good leaders identify the values that they want the team, the products and services, and the customer care to embody. Values are high-level, visionary goals for the impact we want our company to make. They speak to **what we do** as a team and **how we do it.** When we're not hitting our values, other metrics become hit-and-miss. Successes aren't repeated, and achievements can be lost in a heartbeat.

Values seem lofty. Translating them for application takes leadership. It's one thing to say, "Integrity is a high team value here." It's another thing to consistently ask "How are we living out integrity as team members?" This tactic is a way to assess how well your team is embodying values.

Regardless of how vague a value may sound, you'd be shocked how confidently each of your employees can say whether they see the company living out a given value. With clear parameters for what living out the value looks like, their feedback gets even more accurate.

Though you may never take your team for ax throwing, the first retention tactic I want to share is about target checking your values.

## Target Check Your Values:     10 · 5 · 1 Method

## Your Value

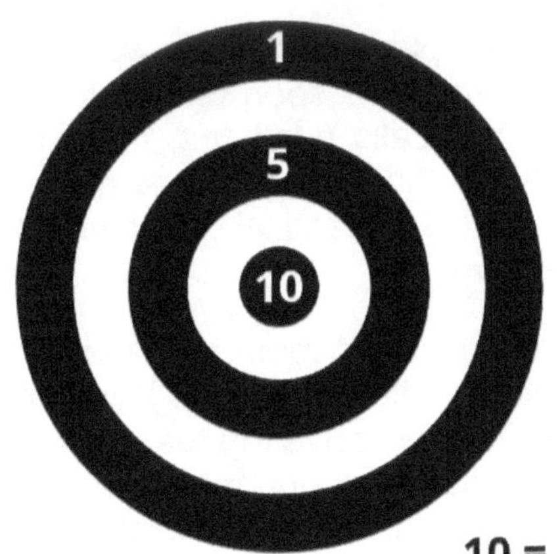

Always discuss the meaning of the score, ideas of what influenced making the score, and what would move it closer to the center.

**10 = Fully Expressed This Value**
**5 = Partly Expressed This Value**
**1 = Completely Missing the Mark**

# How to Target Check Your Values:

1.  Clarify Your Values
2.  Draw a Target
3.  Get Multiple Perspectives
4.  Brainstorm Ideas for Moving Toward the Center


Tactic #1 for retaining the talent on your team is to involve the whole team in evaluating how well the company is embodying core values. To do this, get the team together for a group discussion. Let them know that the goal of the discussion is to get a sense of how you're doing as a team at pursuing the core values for success and thriving as a team.

Facilitate clear feedback by drawing or printing up a set of targets. Label each value that you'd like to check in on, one per target. Set some context for the check-in by describing what each value means. This includes giving examples of the behaviors that model each value. As the leader, it's your responsibility to ask and answer the question: "If this was our value, how would we be acting to model this value? How would we see the value played out day-to-day on the team?"

Don't assume consensus over what your values mean. Create clarity instead.

Unless leaders illustrate how values are played out in the workplace, values end up just being words on the wall. I've seen teams define a value of kindness as meaning "customer calls don't ring more than twice," and a value of accountability as "including errors made in weekend reports rather than hiding them." Get practical about what the value looks like, and the values come alive.

After you finish this discussion, give each team member a marker or push pin, or a turn on the virtual meeting white board, and invite each person up to show how close to center they perceive the team to be on the value in the past ninety days. Give them an opportunity to share what they think is keeping the score from hitting a bullseye, and to suggest something they think could possibly help move things closer to the center in the next 90 days. The goal is creating clarity and making progress, without expecting perfection overnight.

Though team members shouldn't be forced to "solve" the problem before speaking up, every person who notices room for improvement on a value can share some ideas to begin moving in the right direction. With practice, even team members who aren't accustomed to collaborative problem solving can learn to collaborate this way.

Don't expect everyone to score each value the same. Make it clear that different perspectives are expected due to the differences in each person's job description and responsibilities. Ideally, letting everyone weigh in and give ideas of how to move toward the center will spark creativity and illuminate areas of strain or irritation that could become serious problems later.

As you do this, it may be helpful to focus on different contexts for the values you're assessing. Clarify if you want to talk about how the team culture is doing at embodying the core values of the company. Or look at customer experience to see how well the values are translating to customer service and satisfaction. Or if your team puts out a product or digital solution, evaluate how the product lives up to the values set at the heart of your organization.

Just as that ax landing in an outer ring of the target shows room for improvement, the values target check gives a sense of where your team culture, customer satisfaction, and production could be improved.

This is not only true of team members on the "management" staff. Frontline workers and technical staff members have a prime perspective on company culture, customer experience, and operational effectiveness. By involving more team members in checking in on the values, you show them their perspective is valuable, encourage them to take ownership in moving the team forward, and gain insights for how to strengthen everyone's performance as a whole.

Target checking values on a regular basis creates a culture of growth. It reinforces the leadership's vision for company identity and attaches that big vision to daily work.

## Identify Your Core Values

You may be tempted to bypass this step. Please don't. Leading my own life, family, and business from a set of values has helped me make tough decisions and hold myself accountable. They've grounded me so that I can hold others accountable, and advance toward my purpose rather than being sucked into daily chaos. They've helped me make the powerful decision, instead of the easy one. Clarifying values in a tangible way has helped me attract, win, and lead like-minded, like-valued talent to my teams.

Values give us the language to be bold, the clarity to hold fast, and the permission to pivot in pursuit of the true success we need. Values never let us down.

Maybe you're not sure what your company's core values should be or what the real meaning of your company's values are. Below is an exercise to capture the authentic core values you and your organization want to embody. If done right these values can focus your strategy, activate your motivation, and clarify solutions you desperately need. Living your values will help you retain your employees.

Use this exercise when you're ready to make core values power and guide your work. In the pages that follow you'll find a list of values. These are some useful words I've seen at work in many of the companies I've consulted with over the past couple decades.

But know this: this is not a wordsmithing exercise. Picking words that sound good, or speak to the buzz of the cultural moment will not guide your everyday work. This is not about creating a "pretty statement." Though some words may excite you more than others, look for words that define the purpose you are committed to.

At Harbour Resources we recommend hiring an outside consultant to help facilitate this process. Although in-house managers can lead this kind of discussion, outside facilitators can help keep the conversations moving, get everyone involved so one person doesn't dominate the conversations and direction (creating a lack of buy-in) and also bring focus when the team gets stuck. When a leader misses the mark on values, it increases the likelihood of losing values-driven employees.

The goal is to walk away with everyone feeling they have a voice in the direction and everyone is buying in so there is accountability moving forward.


## Core Value Questions

Identify the values that you want to embody as an individual and in your culture. Use these questions to prime your mind for what matters. Reference the list of values, which follows, to get your ideas flowing. These are your values; lead the way in choosing with intention.

☐ If you were to start a new organization/team/family, would you build it around this core value regardless of the industry?

☐ Would you want your organization/team/family to continue to stand for this core value 100 years into the future, no matter what changes occur in the outside world?

☐ Would you want your organization/team/family to hold this core value, even if at some point in time it became a competitive disadvantage—even if in some instances the environment penalized the organization for living this core value?

☐ Do you believe that those who do not share this core value—those who breach it consistently—simply do not belong in your organization?

☐ Would you personally continue to hold this core value even if you were not rewarded for holding it?

☐ Would you change jobs before giving up this core value?

☐ If you awoke tomorrow with more than enough money to retire comfortably for the rest of your life, would you continue to apply this core value to your productive activities?

# Circle 10-20 values that are extremely important to you.

| | | | |
|---|---|---|---|
| Abundance | Curiosity | Imagination | Refinement |
| Acceptance | Daring | Impact | Reflection |
| Accessibility | Decisiveness | Impartiality | Relaxation |
| Accomplishment | Deference | Independence | Reliability |
| Accountability | Delight | Individuality | Relief |
| Accuracy | Dependability | Influence | Reputation |
| Achievement | Depth | Ingenuity | Resilience |
| Acknowledgement | Desire | Inquisitiveness | Resolve |
| Activeness | Determination | Insightfulness | Resourcefulness |
| Adaptability | Devotion | Inspiration | Respect |
| Adoration | Dexterity | Integrity | Responsibility |
| Advancement | Dignity | Intelligence | Rest |
| Adventure | Diligence | Intimacy | Restraint |
| Affection | Direction | Intuition | Reverence |
| Affluence | Directness | Inventiveness | Richness |
| Aggressiveness | Discipline | Investing | Rigor |
| Agility | Discovery | Involvement | Sacredness |
| Alertness | Discretion | Joy | Sacrifice |
| Altruism | Diversity | Justice | Satisfaction |
| Ambition | Dominance | Kindness | Science |
| Amusement | Dreaming | Knowledge | Security |
| Anticipation | Drive | Leadership | Self-control |
| Appreciation | Duty | Learning | Selflessness |
| Approachability | Eagerness | Liberty | Self-reliance |
| Art | Ease | Lightness | Self-respect |
| Articulacy | Economy | Liveliness | Sensitivity |
| Artistry | Efficiency | Logic | Sensuality |
| Assertiveness | Elegance | Longevity | Serenity |
| Assurance | Empathy | Love | Service |
| Attentiveness | Encouragement | Loyalty | Sharing |
| Attractiveness | Endurance | Mastery | Significance |
| Audacity | Energy | Maturity | Silence |
| Availability | Enjoyment | Meaning | Simplicity |
| Awareness | Entertainment | Mellowness | Sincerity |
| Awe | Enthusiasm | Meticulousness | Skillfulness |
| Balance | Ethics | Mindfulness | Solidarity |
| Beauty | Excellence | Modesty | Solitude |
| Being the best | Excitement | Motivation | Sophistication |
| Belonging | Exhilaration | Nature | Speed |
| Benevolence | Expectancy | Neatness | Spirit |
| Bliss | Expediency | Nerve | Spirituality |
| Boldness | Experience | Non-conformity | Spontaneity |
| Bravery | Expertise | Obedience | Stability |
| Brilliance | Exploration | Open- | Stillness |
| Calmness | Expressiveness | mindedness | Strength |
| Camaraderie | Extravagance | Openness | Structure |
| Candor | Fairness | Optimism | Success |

| | | | |
|---|---|---|---|
| Capability | Faith | Order | Support |
| Caring | Fame | Organization | Surprise |
| Carefulness | Family | Originality | Sympathy |
| Celebrity | Fascination | Outdoorsiness | Synergy |
| Certainty | Fashion | Partnership | Teaching |
| Challenge | Fearlessness | Patience | Teamwork |
| Change | Fidelity | Passion | Thankfulness |
| Charity | Fierceness | Peace | Thoroughness |
| Charm | Fitness | Perceptiveness | Thoughtfulness |
| Cheerfulness | Flexibility | Perfection | Thriftiness |
| Clarity | Flow | Perkiness | Tidiness |
| Cleanliness | Focus | Perseverance | Timeliness |
| Cleverness | Fortitude | Persistence | Tranquility |
| Comfort | Frankness | Persuasiveness | Transcendence |
| Commitment | Freedom | Philanthropy | Trust |
| Community | Friendliness | Piety | Trustworthiness |
| Compassion | Friendship | Playfulness | Truth |
| Competence | Frugality | Pleasantness | Understanding |
| Competition | Fun | Pleasure | Unflappability |
| Completion | Generosity | Poise | Uniqueness |
| Composure | Giving | Polish | Unity |
| Concentration | Grace | Popularity | Usefulness |
| Confidence | Gratitude | Potency | Valor |
| Congruency | Growth | Power | Variety |
| Connection | Guidance | Practicality | Victory |
| Conservation | Happiness | Pragmatism | Virtue |
| Consistency | Harmony | Precision | Vision |
| Contentment | Health | Preparedness | Vitality |
| Continuity | Heart | Presence | Vivacity |
| Contribution | Helpfulness | Privacy | Volunteering |
| Control | Heroism | Professionalism | Warm- |
| Conviction | Holiness | Prosperity | heartedness |
| Conviviality | Honesty | Prudence | Warmth |
| Cooperation | Honor | Punctuality | Watchfulness |
| Correctness | Hopefulness | Purity | Willingness |
| Courage | Hospitality | Rationality | Winning |
| Courtesy | Humility | Realism | Wisdom |
| Creativity | Humor | Reason | Wittiness |
| Credibility | Hygiene | Recognition | Wonder |
| | | Recreation | |

## Pick the 6 that are the most important to you and write them here:

1. _______________________   2. _______________________

3. _______________________   4. _______________________

5. _______________________   6. _______________________

Once you have these core team values selected, the next step is to define each one with a clear statement everyone can commit to. Sharpen and put meaning into the dictionary definition to create the team definition. Then identify three to ten behaviors that model this definition. Check out **www.HarbourResources.com** to see how we have done this at Harbour Resources.

Defining values is crucial for creating consensus, building momentum, and enforcing accountability. Without consensus, people may pursue the value in conflicting ways. For example, if you decide teamwork is a core team value but someone thinks being a team player is leading by example and never helping others grow, you will see a block in the transfer of knowledge and skill. If kindness and respect mean never making anyone feel bad, your culture will lack the positive accountability and honest communication needed to overcome barriers and grow. Interrupt chronic frustration and resentment by clarifying the values as a team.

This consensus is also necessary to overcome the conditioning of team members to the values you have. Let's take trust for example. My understanding of trust was forged in an unsafe childhood home. We lived in constant chaos, violence, and abuse. My childhood impacts my conditioning to trust teammates. Someone who would want to lead me in developing a culture of trust can work past my background by defining trust in culture-specific terms, and giving my colleagues and myself defined ways to earn and honor trust in the arena of work. Otherwise, my conditioning could leave me vulnerable to being triggered to operate on my childhood conditioning.

Once you have the definition, you must ask everyone to define the behaviors you will all commit to, to live out the value. This shared commitment to the value forms a basis for positive accountability.

In our example of trust, embodied behaviors could look like:

- Never gossiping or talking about someone behind their back.

- Stopping any teammate who attempts to gossip to me about a coworker.

- Showing up to work on time and fulfilling my designated hours without wasting time cruising the internet while on the clock.

You may be saying this is not important or you don't have time to do this work as a leader. But look around your own work. Do you know the values of your organization? What happens when there are alignment issues? How do you feel inside when you feel like you are being asked to violate a value? This is crucial work for your leadership. Not only will it provide inspiration for your team and overcome destructive forces of dissonance, it will give pathways for accountability and tools for recruiting and interviewing. Do this work. You will be able to target check your team, your interviewing, and your leadership. You will thank me later.

## Why Assessing Values Performance Retains Talent

Turnover results from unkept promises. A low performing employee is fired because they cannot do what their résumé promised. An employee drowns because they never received the support they needed. Layoffs are needed to restructure due to loss of market share. In every circumstance, there was a promise made, but not delivered.

People are surprising; they can push through overwhelming adversity and solve impossible problems. But one thing they can't do indefinitely is live in dissonance. If the company says it values its employees but doesn't keep humane staffing ratios, it will continually lose employees. If the company says respect is a company value but bullying and prejudice run unchecked, it will lose employees. In addition to dissonance in how employees are treated, if the company isn't living out its stated values, then employees get caught between the company and unhappy customers who aren't getting what they were promised either.

Dig into any lost employee—especially the high performers—and I promise you will find dissonance or a lack of follow through on your company values. There are mountains of research about what causes burnout, but a common theme in most of it is a lack of clear direction and connectedness to a purpose or values.[14]

I sometimes talk about the virtue of integrity as being the same, honest self in every room you walk into. But in our companies, integrity means doing the hard work of delivering on an intentional set of values that sit at the beating heart of our companies. A company is not a single person who can "simply be authentic." Coherently living your values as a team is the only way an organization can have integrity. The company takes on the character that is embodied by everyday choices, systematic processes, and the reinforcement of attitudes that honor the values of the organization.

Our company values can elevate us; they can help us play the infinite game and continue building competitive advantage even in challenging seasons. But company values are not an elitist planning exercise for the C-Suite. Employees at every level of the organization need to be involved in living out the values, and assessing how well those values are showing up in the workplace.

## Your Voice Isn't Enough

To uncover the dissonance, and improve your company's ability to embody its values, this can't be a solo exercise. If "living our values" sounds like an intellectual exercise, you're still missing it. Get out some targets, talk to some colleagues, and hear from multiple voices to gain perspective.

For one thing, the people you ask to evaluate the culture need to be listened to, to prompt their ownership and engagement in the company values. Get people thinking about where the team isn't delivering, and what could improve things. Sometimes cultures have a lot of problems to fix before they will become a talent magnet. By listening to the team, you currently have and engaging their feedback on the culture, you earn trust. Having a voice in improving the culture activates the employees' sense of belonging, and brings their unique insights to help your team grow.

If you are not a titled leader, or high up in the executive team, look for a way you can have positive conversations with colleagues about how to more effectively embody the company values you find most meaningful. This can be as simple as saying "Hey (colleague), I know we're supposed to be efficient in dealing with this part of our workload. On a scale of 1-10 how do you think we're doing lately? What went into giving that score? How do you think we could improve the score between the two of us in the next couple weeks?" In that example "efficiency" is the company value, and even in an informal conversation you've drawn a target (scale of 1-10), and gotten curious about what the other person's perspective could do to help you bring more of that value into practice in the weeks to come.

Don't underestimate the value of speaking up when you have the opportunity. It can be tempting to believe nothing ever changes. We can shift into self-protection mode and not even speak up when our leaders ask for our input. Prepare yourself for the next opportunity to contribute to your organization's success. Maybe if you look hard enough, you can find a way right now to help your team see how well they're living out their values, and move toward more integrity in the weeks to come.

## Take Action:

This tactic involves the whole team in assessing how your organization is doing at living out its values. Wherever you are in your organization, there is something you can do to embody the company values and address inconsistencies. Use these action steps as a springboard to imagine more ways to deliver on the culture's promises and retain the talent you already have.

### If You're on the Frontline:

- Make an effort to discover and understand your company's values. Choose a value and talk with a colleague or leader about how you could help each other embody the value more in your day-to-day work.

- Don't shut down when you notice the company failing to live a value out; look for ways to get help from team members or leaders to challenge the inconsistency and move the company in a positive direction.

### If You're a Manager or Supervisor:

- Choose some company values to focus on with your team, and get a good handle on what living out each value looks like for those you lead (and yourself!) This is defining those values in terms of workload, and forms a base for integrity. Discuss these definitions and gain feedback from your team as a foundation for target checks and growth.

- Print up targets and hold a Values Check Meeting; walk your team through this process, and gain insights from as many voices as possible on how you as a team can deliver on promises to the customer and to one another.

**If You're an Executive Leader:**

- Don't let your company values die in the C-Suite closet. Get them out and help your management team live out these values toward the employees and your clients.

- Get outside the chain of management for perspective on how well your organization is delivering on your values. Facilitate wide-scale target checks, or at least get input from every level of the organization to ground your perspective in the lived experience of all employees.

# Retention Tactic #2:
## *Build a S.T.A.Y. Program*

Employees want to feel like they have a future. They do not want to be enslaved by the daily grind of the company's goals without some development of their talent and potential. Research shows us the number one reason an employee decides to stay or leave their employer is related to their development and growth. Money is still only the fourth or fifth priority decision-making factor for staying or leaving a job.

Think about it like this, if you were a beginner snow skier would you want to be continuously beat up by the work of skiing, or would you want to be coached and taught how to get better so it becomes easier and more enjoyable?

Do you want your job as a leader to become easier? If you said yes, then the best thing you can do is develop the people on your team so they can take your place, versus them just feeling like they are doing your job.

Most companies do ad-hoc development to triage the problems created by a lack of system. Then again, once enough mistakes are made, customer complaints threaten the bottom line and bookkeeping errors or inappropriate conduct cause liability concerns, those employees will be fired or developed. But crisis-level training to fix serious issues isn't the kind of employee development that draws the best out of employees. Leaders often blame people for what is actually the lack of a system for developing employees.

At other workplaces, haphazard growth opportunities are offered whenever a manager or leader gets excited about some system or process. But how many of us have been involved with random, short-lived learning initiatives and knew it wouldn't make a difference? "This too shall pass" is how our employees react to our growth initiatives if they know the initiatives are the flavor of the month.

In the rest of the book, we will outline two major systems that allow talent to S.T.A.Y. with you. To do that, we combine a Universal Training Pathway (UTP) with an Individual Development Plan (IDP) in a single S.T.A.Y. Development Process that will revolutionize your talent retention. This process actually starts in the Attraction phase and continues through the entire life cycle of the employee at your company.

Let's start with what S.T.A.Y. stands for:

**S**ystematic

**T**ransferrable

**A**chieves Mastery

**Y**ou-Focused


The S.T.A.Y. Development Process is a SYSTEMATIC process of TRANSFERRING culture and ACHIEVING MASTERY through a YOU-FOCUSED personal development plan.

We start with this mindset as the key to creating a company where employees want to stay. Practical tools like a talent identification scorecard, onboarding checklist, equipping plans, and accountability strategies only work as well as the mindset that created them.

Do you systematically implement the strategy you use in a way that lets your organization learn and innovate? Do managers and leaders see the interconnecting ways each department and role fits into the larger system of the company? Does the work you do to equip or strengthen one employee amplify value by being passed on and on in an effective way? Are the humans working in your company getting more masterful, more effective, and more expert? Do your employees feel seen, valued, and supported as individuals while they are serving your company's mission?

Use the Mindset Check-In the Take Action section for this tactic and let the S.T.A.Y. acrostic uncover the deficits in your current company's approach to employee development.

## Build a Universal Training Pathway

Create a structure and development process that has a tangible rhythm in your workplace. Whether it's micro-masterminds that happen for one lunch break a month, quarterly elective options for skills development, or a coaching program in place for all employees, this established rhythm of growth enriches the value of your workplace and helps you rise above competitors.

Reach beyond the basics of helping your employees acquire the minimum skills to complete their work. Development isn't just a phase of onboarding. Employee development will indeed help your employees do their jobs better every day. But the object of development reaches beyond filling in deficiencies. Ongoing development extends and broadens the team member's value by elevating their skills and capacities as far as they're capable, without stopping when their functional capacity reaches "adequate." When we make development and growth a part of our culture, employees start looking for areas to innovate and improve in their work without us having to ask all the time.

Some employers fail to take the ceiling off of their employees' development, and become vulnerable to losing their best performers when they've achieved the employer's expectations in their role. If instead, performing well was extended by further development, those high achievers could keep growing and expanding their value to your organization indefinitely.

## Employ Individual Development Plans

Creating a universal training pathway (UTP) for all employees is a great foundation for lifting the workforce in unison. It may even strengthen cohesion in the culture, and decrease barriers created by differences in knowledge. But what it won't do is help each individual team member become all that they can be. For that you need to implement Individual Development Plans (IDP) for each employee to help them gain mastery and thrive in life and work.

A UTP may take a technical engineer and continuously raise their technical expertise. But what if that individual has divergent interests? What if given options, they would strengthen their communication skills? Or learn strategic planning? Or want to dabble with design elements only to find they have incredibly innovative ideas emerge from their long stint on the technical side of life?

Personalizing the development of each of your employees means caring about who they're becoming, not just what actions they're doing. Some of the most successful organizations have pivoted and kept a viable margin during seasons of global upheaval because they've had high internal worker mobility. Resilient companies move the talent of staff around their organizations. If you allow the unique gifts of your employees to grow, they become capable of enriching more and more parts of your company in new and different ways.

The Universal Training Pathway (UTP) helps companies become more cohesive and reliably excellent. The Individual Development Plan (IDP) allows the uniqueness of each employee to flourish and expand to their fullest potential. Together they give your company durability and innovation, consistency and contrasting strengths all working together to safeguard your company's success in an uncertain and rapidly changing world.

## Dealing With Losing Talent

One of the strongest hesitations most leaders have about developing the talent of their employees is the fear that employees will outgrow them. Perhaps your organization doesn't have built-in advancement opportunities. What if too much development leads to your employee leaving for the next company?

For some of our organizations, this risk seems serious. But at the root of this concern is a blind spot that most of us have; we think our employees can stay as they are.

It's as if we see developing our staff and watching them grow and change as one option, and the other option is to let them keep being as good as they are right now forever.

But they won't. Think about your own career. Did you stay just the same as you languished in a dead-end position? Have you been forced to leapfrog the limitations of your current role to grow at a different company? Maybe you've become used to this chronic stagnation and think starting your own company is the only way to have limitless growth potential.

Like a muscle that can grow with intelligent use, your employees will strengthen if you deploy their energy intelligently. But if you don't, the muscles of their potential will atrophy and die. Our lowest performers are often exactly these people, atrophied and trudging away with dwindling vitality. Don't resent employees who leave to grow when your lack of a growth pathway gives them no other option.

Many of our companies are filled with burned out employees. Having workers stay with us "forever" is only a positive thing if they're vital and engaged. Smart leaders are creating work environments where applicants learn "we'll develop you while you're here. If you join us, you will grow." This leverages human nature in a powerful way, and will certainly help you attract more strong employees in today's more mobile global economy.

If you are the kind of company where entry-level talent is all that's needed in many roles, you might create a strategic advantage by becoming known as the best company to get your start in, a place where you can bring your energy and develop until you're ready to go.

## Grow Into Employee Development

When I talk to leaders about developing their people in a more strategic, ongoing way, they often push back with cost concerns. So, let's talk frankly about the costs associated with developing your people.

First, employee development only looks expensive when we compartmentalize development costs away from our essential Human Resources budget. Take a serious look at the financial impacts of your turnover. Talent loss is an astronomical proportion of your avoidable expenses.

Most of us don't want to take radical ownership of our team, their engagement, and their turnover rates. We want to blame the talent loss on the employee and call them the wrong hire. But I'll share with you what I share with my clients: even if you hire the right person in the beginning, if you don't challenge and help them grow they will become the wrong person eventually.

We need everyone on our teams to keep growing and learning to keep up with their potential. So, whether the employees who leave never were the right person, or they became the wrong person through stagnation, the cost of losing them may well have been avoidable. Let's pre-invest the budget for future employee loss into developing team members.

Second, if your team is in real trouble, you may have to pry open the profitability and performance of your team strategically and slowly. To do this, look for small forms of stable, ongoing, personalized employee development. It takes time to turn the ship to energize and activate your team. But get creative and see what you can build in today. Create a foundation of development that starts new hires off right, and set serious goals to increase your investment in development over time. And don't wait to get expert help. Even companies like mine have resources for all budgets.

## MicroLearning–not Microwave Learning

Most companies need to blend the MacroLearning of intensive training, workshops, and coaching with a MicroLearning structure that keeps enriching their talent in small doses. If you've already got the big training structure in place, great; use MicroLearning to massage those skills and culture values into your team. But if you don't have the time, space, or budget to do a massive MacroLearning initiative, start with MicroLearning first.

Get creative to schedule ten-minute learning and training sessions. Sometimes fifteen or thirty minutes of learning together at regular intervals can provide a foundation for momentum in your talent development. But there is a difference between random, ad-hoc training to address each random problem as it comes up. I call this "microwave training" where a problem or new opportunity inspires you to try to "zap" some energy or information into your team.

Often this hit-and-run learning feels like punishment. Perhaps one team member made a costly mistake; so we schedule an hour of mandatory training for everyone. Instead of strengthening the team, the individual who made the mistake feels scapegoated and everyone else feels punished along with them.

MicroLearning is a way of allowing consistent space to cover material in a strategic way. Work through the skills or information you want to pass to the team in small bites. Review and revisit information to help massage the practices and techniques into the team culture so they can take root. Get your people together consistently, teach them to grow together, and the talent quotient on your teams will rise.

If you aren't in a position to institute a full structure of MicroLearning at your organization, take an individual approach. Look for opportunities in coaching or mentoring conversations—or even collaborative conversations with colleagues—to focus on increasing your personal mastery, or the team's effectiveness around something.

Most things worth changing won't change in a day. But I've never met a day where there wasn't some small action I could take that would eventually add up to meaningful change.

We teach our clients to use an onboarding checklist as the MicroLearning plan to create small sessions in small doses each month to upskill or level set expectations. Another idea we recommend is the use of podcasts or videos where everyone listens or watches and then has roundtable discussions to learn perspectives from the team. In the fitness world this is called HIIT or High Intensity Interval Training—a short burst then a break. Training doesn't have to be an hour or a day long. We must rethink the two-day workshops and reshape them into

MicroLearning sessions. At Harbour Resources, we provide the in-depth sessions but then back them up with online and virtual micro-training.

## Learning Cohorts for Healthcare Teams

Healthcare and other twenty-four seven industries have a unique challenge for training. To some extent, remote teams also have challenges as the global spread of employees means that getting everyone on the team learning time together may be impossible.

If this is your company, then finding effective ways to learn together is more important than ever. Solve the problem of scheduling growth time together by crafting learning cohorts. Divide your teams according to schedule dynamics and/or time zone.

It takes work as a leader to master logistics. It may also require rethinking staffing schedules to build more team stability and cohesion. Teams where schedules and employees switch shifts and locations continuously tend to have lower continuity of knowledge and slower growth. Teams that build up their teamwork experience and knowledge of their coworkers' strengths and expertise outperform the mishmash team of whoever-showed-up-today.

I challenge you to make the effort to develop structure for continuous improvement through learning. This is the kind of leadership today's world of work demands.


**Recruitment Bonus: Outshine Other Employers**

Restaurant owner Lori waited for the jet that would carry her on the final leg home, chatting with me when her mobile buzzed. Seeing it was one of her employees, she answered and kicked her heels up on the carryon at her feet.

I'm not a nosy man, but sitting across from her impromptu office, I listened to the helping half of a fifteen-minute, personal development mentoring session between the owner of a company and one of the dozens of employees in her care. Was Lori answering questions about how to handle work problems? Reporting on a problem with the restaurant inventory system? No. Lori offered help on getting their first mortgage.

When was the last time your manager invested in helping you navigate a personal growth challenge or overcome a barrier in your personal life? If it's happened at all, you remember that manager. You were also more likely to work hard, feel valued, and stay resilient during work challenges while you worked for them.

If you build a S.T.A.Y. Development Program it will not only help you keep the employees you have, it will also make your company compelling to the top talent when you need to recruit. If you want to attract the kind of employees who will continually enrich and grow your organization, you need self-motivated learners who seek personal mastery. Attract them by building a systematic, ongoing, and personalized development program.

Your employment brand needs to show through to employee prospects. By systematizing your S.T.A.Y. Development Process, you can communicate it to candidates who apply for your organization. In today's highly mobile workforce, this provides a durable incentive for employee loyalty and engagement.

Employers have to compete to get the best talent out there. How people can expect to be developed while they work for you can provide the competitive hiring advantage your company needs to be able to win the competition. These non-monetary benefits also help companies balance salary costs while enriching the talent pool they have already acquired.

## Take Action:

This tactic was all about developing people in a way that helps talent S.T.A.Y. at your organization. Wherever you are in your organization, there is something you can do to participate in the system of development, transfer knowledge on to others, achieve mastery for yourself, and keep growing as an individual. Here are some action steps as examples. Use them as a springboard to imagine more ways to fulfill your own potential at work and help others do the same.

**If You're on the Frontline:**

- Investigate what growth and learning opportunities are currently available at your company. If none exist, discuss with your leader what it could look like for you to get more support or input on expanding your skills, systematizing your workload, or planning for some personally rewarding achievement in your role. Having your own Individual Development Plan (IDP) can reduce your burnout and increase the value you add at your company.

- Practice *sapere vedere* for your own life. Where do you see yourself growing or needing to grow? What are you wanting to achieve? Set some goals for the next decade and map the steps you could take at work or in your personal life to help you get there. If you can, hire a coach to elevate your growth.

**If You're a Manager or Supervisor:**

- Reflect on the team members under your care and make a list of the values, skills, or behaviors you want to see them being able to transfer to others. Make a plan to assess how well they have received what you want them to embody, and ask how they can be more ready to pass it on to others. Begin coaching your employees consistently on a monthly basis and work with them to empower growth.

- Learning happens through repetition. Outline the ten most important values, behaviors, or skills you want to see used on your team and take one each work day for two weeks, to look for a way to reinforce each one of them over and over again. At the end of ten weeks, assess where you have seen improvements and consider reformulating a new list of ten things to focus on equipping and reinforcing with your team.

**If You're an Executive Leader:**

- Take a serious look at your company's learning and growth system. Does it represent a faulty firehose, or is it a consistent sprinkler system? Review the elements of S.T.A.Y. (**S**ystematic, **T**ransferrable, **A**chievement of Mastery, **Y**ou-Focused for the employee) and see where your company has work to do.

- What are the ways your company supports and develops your employees as individuals? Professional development is important, but to compete for and unlock the potential of the best workers today, your company will need to help them thrive as humans outside of work as well. Take the time to evaluate some small ways your company could help your employees thrive away from work and build a pathway to implement them in the next twelve months.

## Extended Resources

At Harbour Resources we offer training and coaching specifically around our QLT Cultural Framework, as well as provide online and virtual on-demand leadership videos, podcasts, and articles to assist leaders and companies in developing their teams. Learn more at **HarbourResources.com**.

# Retention Tactic #3:
## *Engage Tactical Praise*

With the stress and pressure of our economy, employees are more ready than ever to be happy and settled at a company that appreciates their work. Before you lose good employees to burnout and your competition, try giving them a Praise Raise.

Most workers who leave their jobs go because they don't feel appreciated and trusted by their direct supervisor. By offering genuine praise, you strengthen the relationship your employees have to the company, and reinforce praiseworthy behaviors. When done right, all levels of the team management engage in giving genuine feedback and honest praise. Companies who do this drastically reduce employee loss.

It doesn't cost anything to give employees a Praise Raise. Research on employee retention suggests this raise is the one your team is looking for anyway. Don't resign yourself to the expensive proposition of replacing people simply because you can't afford to pay them more to stay. Give them a bonus that will keep them coming to work with increasing enthusiasm in the months ahead.

When I talk about Tactical Praise I sometimes get raised eyebrows. I think some people see praise as a way of manipulating people, trying to force trust, or "kissing up" so that you can get more of what you want from people.

But I have a military background. I know that powerful equipment needs skill, intelligence, and careful practice if it's going to be effective and safe. Praise is one of the most powerful tools in any leader's arsenal. Most leaders who fail to be tactical, intentional, and skilled with praise aren't being more sincere; they're failing to respect the meaning and impact that their words and silences have.

In this section, we'll look at how to give Tactical Praise. But before we do, let's look at three kinds of praise that backfire. They represent three misuses of the power of praise.

# Three Kinds of Toxic Praise

1.  **Vague Praise**

2.  **Celebratory Praise**

3.  **Comparative Praise**

### Toxic Praise #1: Vague Praise

First let's talk about Vague Praise. Like striding through a crowd waving a gun around, this kind of noisy, hot-air praise may get some attention, but it won't be the positive kind. As has been seen in companies with a "just say thank you" campaign dictated by upper management, empty words of vague appreciation tend to backfire.[8]

Here's what vague praise sounds like:

- Thanks for all you do here!

- Way to go team!

- Good job everyone!

On the surface, it doesn't sound harmful at all. But more often than not those words of praise are offered to smooth over unreasonable demands, unstable leadership, or obliviousness from managers who don't comprehend the work their team does.

When vague praise is used as icing on the cake of a stressed leader's rudeness, a Band-Aid on the job insecurity everyone is feeling, or to try to put on a positive face in front of their own superiors, the team is more likely to be offended than validated.

To identify vague praise, use the Speed Test. One way to know if you are giving vague, lazy praise is to look at how fast it is delivered and moved on from. Take the first example of vague praise in this chapter: "Thank you for all you do here." When the manager tosses it over their shoulder on the way out the door, it's not positive. By contrast, what if that same leader took a few minutes during their lunch break to stop by in between your projects, waited until you were done with your current project or phone call, and said "Hey Alex, thanks for all you do here."

It's like going through the office and giving people pens. Thrown fast, it's a threat, an interruption, an irritation. But when you walk up to someone, wait until they're able to give you their attention, and offer it to them gently in your hand, they can take it as a gift.

If you think the praise you're giving your team is quality, but it's at risk of seeming vague and lazy, test your pace of delivery. If it passes the speed test, you're conveying more meaning with your patience and delivery. By slowing down, you escape the laziness quotient.

If you carve out a real conversational space to offer your unspecific praise to someone in, you're more likely to spontaneously expand on the praise by explaining why you're telling them, and how you've seen them be a praiseworthy teammate. As in our example with Alex's boss, after getting Alex's attention and saying "thanks for all you do here," the very space created by waiting for Alex to be able to listen prompts the boss to say more. "I can tell you try to make sure your team members have what they need," or "You bring a lot of consistency to the team," or "I like the new idea you suggested in this week's meeting." Because there is meaning within the praise, slowing down naturally leads to communicating more of that meaning.

But more on the good kind of praise later.

For now, it's important to recognize that laziness in your efforts to praise always backfire. Your team isn't a stranger you sit next to on an airplane once; they see you over, and over, and over again. Praise draws on a dynamite core of affirmation and notices the value of an individual as a human. When you let your praise get vague, it becomes dehumanizing. Stop this kind of toxic "thank you" immediately. If your praise doesn't connect, it alienates. If you need conversation starters, or help building the connection to slow down with your colleagues, check out the C2 Rounding Practice taught in Activation Tactic #4.

For example, Ochsner Baptist Hospital CEO Beth Walker makes time to write handwritten gratitude notes to employees. The way she focuses on specific praise for people's attitudes, efforts and ingenuity is what makes her praise an amplifier for success in the organization. I see this with great leaders; they don't make excuses about their full schedule; they make time for acts of genuine praise to feed energy into their organizations.

## Toxic Praise #2: Celebratory Praise

Believe it or not, praising people for their accomplishments actually backfires. Don't just trust me on this, there's a whole body of research behind the psychology of praise and performance in motivational research.[17] Let's summarize it so you can get to using it.

Accomplishments are outside of people's full control. When we praise people for things outside of their control, they become increasingly vulnerable to failure, they cut back on creative innovation, and they avoid positive risk taking. To spur repetition, avoid praise for anything a person cannot repeat.

Examples of Accomplishments Outside Our Control:

- **Signing a New Client/Contract:** the client's decision isn't inside even the best sales person's control.

- **Revenue Growth:** so many factors influence revenue. We like this metric because it has great meaning; but it is not a metric truly inside any person's "control."

- **Customer Satisfaction Scores:** This is something to be celebrated, but the way you praise this can either increase or decrease your employee's efforts in this area.

One of the biggest things that Tactical Praise can do is boost achievement and high performance. The right kind of praise absolutely does have a direct impact on metrics like revenue, satisfaction scores, and new business growth.

But praising uncontrollable outcomes fast tracks stress and burnout *especially in our high performers*. Smart, driven employees know they've combined work and luck to win. How can they be certain their luck will hold? They can't. So they ride the anxiety train. They can feel like they're spinning a roulette wheel every time they go into work since they're fighting for things beyond their power.

## Toxic Praise #3: Comparative Praise

There's a way to praise one person that undermines others. It lifts one person up at the expense of others, but often sounds positive while you're doing it. It's what human potential expert Shawn Achor calls "comparison praise."

Comparative Praise sounds something like this:

- "That was the best presentation I heard all day!"

- "Way to go making this the best quarter in years!"

- "You're faster than anyone else on the team!"

Do those sentences still sound positive to you? Let's unpack them. When you tell someone that their presentation, spreadsheet, or pitch was "the best out of all of them," you're really saying that everyone else's was not as good. It makes their "bestness" dependent on the "worseness" of others. In addition to cutting down others, research shows that this form of praise also increases fear of failure, and reduces positive innovation and healthy risk-taking behaviors among employees.

This kind of praise causes people to slow down their skill acquisition and what experts call "challenge behavior." Challenge behavior is what someone does when they attempt to do something new, or more difficult than what they've easily conquered before. Challenge behavior is crucial to high-performing teams because raising the level of difficulty means boosting our ability to outperform ourselves as time goes on.

When we only praise someone for being "better than the rest" they are incentivized to keep competing at the lower levels, to only take on opportunities that they're certain they can be the "best" at. Though there's nothing wrong with staying in your own area of expertise, the best way to become increasingly exceptional is to surround yourself with people who know more, have more experience, and are ahead of you in those ways. An employee who was praised for being better than everyone else at a small local expo might avoid attending a regional expo and trying to represent their company among the "big fish" presenters who have more experience.

Does your company benefit from staying in its comfort zone? Not usually. But employees make the choice every day to keep finding small enough ponds that they can be the biggest fish in them. One way they may do this is by running off teammates who "show them up" by being better than they are at certain tasks.

I see this in companies all the time. This huge source of brain drain comes from employees fighting to be at the top of the pile. Sure, you need to get rid of bullies in the workplace if they're harassing new high performers who threaten them. But you also need to take ownership if your praise style rewards this toxic outcome.

Comparative praise boosts "cover your bases" excuse-making, and amplifies blaming when things go wrong. It also creates resentment and negative vulnerability among colleagues. So, as you work to increase the praise coefficient at your organization, steer clear of praise that compares altogether. Instead, find ways to praise someone's quality, quickness, or participation in the high performance of the team without comparing them to anyone else.

You might be surprised how much of the praise you give is comparative in nature. Try to notice this week as you go about your life at home and work on the team. Move away from comparison and see what happens.

## Give Tactical Praise

Tactical Praise starts with noticing and communicating the value you see in someone else in the form of their choices, behaviors, attitudes, and efforts. In part, praise improves performance because people start seeing the connection between their choices and the positive feedback they're getting.

Disengaged employees feel that none of their best efforts are really noticed or valued. They stop putting out new ideas because they're ignored or penalized. They pull back their efforts because they've left it all on the court in the past and didn't even receive a "thank you." They may notice others who don't try very hard, who cut corners but keep coloring inside the lines, getting the same compensation as they do, and decide it's time to keep their heads down and just get through the day.

When your employees are disengaged, that low level of performance leads to backlog, mistakes, and overall underperformance for your company. Turn this around by halting disengagement at the root. Start noticing them with tactical praise.

## Praise for Attitude, Effort, and Strategies

Tactical praise affirms one of the three major things that are within each employee's power: their attitude, the effort they make, and their strategic planning or processes they develop.

Praising someone's attitude has a sharper impact the more observantly and precisely you do it. "Thanks for being great to work with" might sound nice, but it isn't very clear. By contrast, saying "thanks for having a sense of humor when everything seemed to go wrong today" affirms the attitude in a way that signals you welcome their continued good humor.

"Wait," you may want to say. "What do I do if everyone has a bad attitude? Nothing to praise around my office right now!" Sometimes it can be tough to find anything to praise. But I challenge you to run a small experiment. Get curious, and start looking for hints of positive attitude factors by hunting for some of the following attitudes at work. Use it like a game of Positive Attitude "I Spy."

## Positive Attitudes:
- Thoughtfulness / Reflection
- Precision or Accuracy
- Attention to Detail
- Attention to Social Energy (reading the room)
- Compassion or Empathy
- Willingness to Change (even if not graciously)
- Voicing Truth (even if unpleasant)
- Restraint
- Calmness
- Going with the Flow
- Acknowledging Others/Greeting
- Gathering Thoughts Before Speaking
- Looking For Possible Flaws/Problems
- Intensity
- Tenacity (even if regarding something you'd rather they let go)

That list is designed to include potentially positive attitude descriptors from all the major temperaments. Some of them will look obviously positive to you, but others will not fit your own temperament. We often fail to praise positive traits like tenacity, voicing the truth, or attention to detail when they're done with an attitude we don't enjoy. But if the tenacity, truth, or attention is there, praising it has the potential to shift the attitude and energy around that trait.

Take a beat and think about it; if you can find any shadow of these and affirm them, you will have a starting spot to turn the negative vibe in your organization around. If the attitude is already bad, you've got nothing to lose, so I hope you give it a try!

## Getting More of People's Best

Addressing negative attitudes is important. But it's even more important to make an effort to praise the positive traits and efforts already on display. Our attention sticks to the low performers, negative members, and squeaky wheels on the team because they irritate us. But sometimes that means all of our attention is absorbed by those team members.

Taking time for activities like coaching and mentoring your functional and strong employees is critical to energizing and increasing their performance. Don't lose the people you value most because they don't realize how much you value them! Even celebrating victories doesn't translate to making the individual employee feel seen and valued.

When that person is being noticed for something they can control, the reward of praise strengthens that employee's motivation to repeat their effort, positivity, or innovation. What gets celebrated gets replicated! So praise as often as possible. But remember, authentic praise is not manipulative.

Praise good attributes to show your gratitude. Praise good attitudes to get more of them. In our Quit Losing Talent Culture Playbook, we offer an employee engagement card. We recommend knowing the birthdate and work anniversary date of every employee. You can use these two dates as a trigger to praise each employee, but build on them. Make it a regular part of your leadership culture to notice and praise employees yourself; then teach your employees how to praise each other as well.

# Take Action:

This tactic is all about praising people in a way that reinforces their confidence and energy, strengthening their sense of being valued at work. Wherever you are in your organization, there is something you can do to help team members feel more valued for their attitudes, efforts, and strategies. Use these action steps to imagine more ways to escape vague, celebratory, or comparative praise.

### If You're on the Frontline:

- Look for ways to praise your teammates. Look for the good in all they do and share this with them, the team, and your boss. Be sincere and make this a regular habit, not just when you want their help.

- If you aren't getting the right kind of praise from your boss, ask for a private meeting and share with them what you feel like you are doing well and let them know you need to hear from them once in a while if you are on track.

### If You're a Manager or Supervisor:

- Use our C-Squared Rounding and Talent Lock conversation tools to consistently connect with and engage your employees and praise the work they are doing. Be sincere and follow the ideas in this tactic so you don't do damage with praise.

- In your coaching sessions with your employees, ask how they like to be recognized and do this for them. Some like being praised in front of others, while others prefer private words. Praise is a skill; if you aren't strong yet, get strong through practice.

### If You're an Executive Leader:

- Make note of forms of toxic praise common in your organization. Replace systems and habits that perpetuate vague, celebratory, or comparative praise and establish tactical praise instead. Praise repeatable actions inside someone's control, and never as a comparison with others.

- Title doesn't replace the need to be valued. High level managers, C-Suite, or department leaders need to be appreciated and praised just as much as frontline workers do. Make it a priority. What you practice, they will practice.

# Retention Tactic #4:
## *Build Equity, Not Equality*

If your organization has turnover problems, you are at risk of seeing everyone as expendable, and to stop seeing people as individuals who deserve to be treated as the unique team member they are. Seeing employees as interchangeable cogs in a machine accelerates turnover.

Think about it for a second. What exactly is your company without the workers that make up your team? An empty call center? A warehouse of goods? A digital platform without content, traffic, or growth? Sick patients needing care? Small business contracts with no one to execute them?

You don't have to be a jerk to create an unfair work environment. Many well-intentioned managers fall into the trap of thinking they have to "treat everyone the same." Have you found yourself uttering those words? Do you pride yourself on a kind of "equality" that doesn't show favoritism by bending the rules or listening to sob stories? If this is you, then fairness and justice may be some of your core leadership values. Good for you.

But beware. Even the fairest leaders can unintentionally disadvantage workers if they don't develop an *equitable* workplace, instead of just an *equal* one.

Different employees have different skills, strengths, and social constraints. Some come from peaceful homes with social support that makes it easy for them to comply with your company's policies on punctuality, professional dress, and responsiveness during off hours.

But some of your employees have to overcome barriers not felt by their colleagues in order to show up in the same way.

Visualize two approaches to dealing with a barrier. One treats everyone the same (equality) in an effort at *fair treatment*. The other treats everyone equitably in an effort at *fair outcomes*.

If by equality we mean treating everyone the same, this means blindness to the barriers our teams are facing. Whether a traditional disability such as vision impairment, or social burdens of caregiving for an aging parent, or unreliable transportation, that barrier makes our "equal treatment" of employees inequitable.

With the 2020 pandemic we recognized the need for parents with young kids to overcome the sudden circumstances of school closures. The whole team profited from accommodating those workers even if we couldn't extend the same options to all other team members.

And when it isn't crisis mode, aim your accommodations to help every employee to pursue the meaningful things in their lives. Like the Boston Consulting Group's (BCG) extensive experimentation with giving high level consultants one dedicated day off every week, the goal was to help each employee have the meaningful kind of time off that uniquely supported their thriving and fulfillment in and out of the workplace.

Universal accommodations such as childcare or anniversary gifts don't apply to the single, non-parents on your staff. The Harvard Researchers working with BCG saw incredible success with a universally honored goal of every individual on the team having the meaningful time off that helped them flourish; and the colleagues worked together as a team to help them have that time. Rules of "treat everyone the same" could prohibit a team from giving all Wednesday mornings off to one team member who wanted to take a special class offered at that time "unless everyone can get Wednesday morning off." But would it even be fair to make everyone take Wednesday morning off so that your team has "fairness?" No. Do the harder and more rewarding work of providing equitable treatment, helping everyone win.

I've heard of creative leaders restoring equitable treatment to the nursing staff at their facilities by instituting strategies like "the Cinderella Shift." With the patient acuity and staffing ratios at their facility, day nurses were more likely than anyone else to be unable to take a real lunch break. While consistent shifts might look fair, real equity meant finding a way to let nurses consistently recharge with a lunch break. The Cinderella Shift at some facilities is a 4-hour staffing shift to allow a rotation of nurses to all take a humane lunch break.

How many employees will you burn out before you explore ways to meet their needs at work? I'm inspired every day by watching managers and leaders step up to make small changes that dramatically improve their staff's endurance and fulfillment.

## Eliminate Barriers to Helping

Most bosses and managers know there are things they can do to help their employees perform at their best. Giving a boost or accommodation to employees strategically can unlock productivity and amplify performance on the team we have. Sometimes this reduces our need for increased staffing, reduces avoidable burnout, and can speed up achievement.

So why don't we as leaders make the accommodations and strategic investments to make our employees' lives easier? More often than not, it's due to pursuing fairness through equality, meaning being willing to do for everyone what you do for anyone.

If I've heard it once I've heard it a thousand times: "if I do that for her, I'll have to do it for everyone. I can't give that employee a twenty-minute grace period on arrival time and still consider them as punctual if I won't give that grace period to everyone."

But there's a problem with globalizing all accommodations across your team; doing this doesn't level the playing field for employees unless everyone is starting off in the same position. I have yet to work on a team where everyone has the same advantages, resources, limitations, and challenges as everyone else.

## Justice Paradigms

Why is it our job as managers and leaders to elevate team members so they can overcome limitations and barriers to work? Depending on your leadership values, you'll be rewarded for the following reasons:

**The Pragmatic Manager:**

If you have an eye for boosting ROI of overhead and resources, creative barrier busting is a power tactic you want to learn. Effectively and intentionally doing this has the bonus benefit of cultivating loyalty in staff, and activates motivation in employees who see that this workplace offers them the support they need to earn more and create greater value than other employers do. This reduction in overhead, and retention and deepening of your talent pool energizes that return on your payroll dollars. The pragmatic reason to seek equity is that it amplifies innovation, reduces talent loss, and expands the resilience of your organization.

**The Moral Manager:**

If you care about justice and value the well-being of the people in your organization, working for equity for your employees serves some of your deepest values. This reduces your own burnout, and helps you build a legacy of meaning at work. Injustice is widespread in our global community, and the workplace is uniquely suited to moving us toward a flourishing future that everyone can enjoy. The moral reason to reduce barriers is because it helps create a more just and humane world for all of us.

**The Achieving Manager:**

The limitations on your achievements are lifted as you successfully empower your team. Simply treating everyone the same doesn't pull everyone together; but treating people as individuals and helping them bring their best to work creates a heightened productive potential. More than that, lowering barriers makes highly diverse teams possible, clearing the way for diversity of thinking, expertise, and experience. Without diversity of thought, it's hard to anticipate and respond to threats, and innovation is risky and slow. In order to achieve through innovation and flexibility, you need to enable very different individuals to come together and perform at their best. The achieving reason to reduce barriers is because it helps your team win.

Maybe you are all three of these managers. If you're going to thrive as a leader, you need to find your way through the minefield of fairness and learn how to lower barriers for the individuals you are charged with leading.

# Strategic Reflection:

**What Accommodations Could or Should I be Making?**

If you're like most of us, you've been trying to meet the stated goal of your job description while following the rules and best practices handed to you by predecessors and bosses. You've been focused on compliance. But to unlock the success potential in your workplace, you'll need to step into a leadership mindset and think outside of what's already expected. Spend some time answering these questions to jumpstart your thinking, and prime your brain to find accommodations worth making for colleagues and employees.

1. **Who on the team is struggling to meet expectations?**

   List them and consider what barriers they are facing when they attempt to meet those expectations. Do they have more to overcome than their colleagues? What's making it harder for them to do what others find easy? Would shadowing them at work, or asking them curious questions help you answer this question more accurately?

2. **Who on the team has been labeled as having a "bad attitude" or "not fitting in here"?**

   List them and consider if there might be unconscious bias put on them because of accepted stereotypes. Fighting bias is one of the barriers you can help address by being intentional and discerning. We all have biases; your character is determined by your efforts to become aware of and address the bias.

3. **Who on the team is making mistakes?**

   Some mistakes show a lack of care, but others point toward a need for training and development. One of the most common barriers I see to employees performing with excellence occurs when their training or onboarding is fast-tracked or poorly executed. It's all too common for teams to have employees with major holes in their knowledge and expertise simply because they didn't have the help and accountability to reach mastery. Sometimes the barrier one team member has is the lack of training of a colleague who is leaning on them too much. Look for these barriers to success and eliminate them by giving the training and coaching needed.

I have said a few times in this book: correct the process before blaming people. But if we're not going to simply blame and cancel people, we need a system to help the people that we have continuously get better. If you're working to create an equitable workplace, you need a viable way to meet people where they are, to pull down inequitable barriers to their participation in the workplace, and then to build their strengths and mastery so that their value and capacity continues to grow.

To put it another way, equity doesn't simply mean leaving everyone as they are and accepting their limitations. It means working hard to reach past unjust limitations to challenge them to grow. Do this with every employee in your company using the Five-Step Equipping Process.

# The Five-Step Equipping Process

In the Army, I learned the "see one, do one, teach one" method of development. My leader would show me how to do something, then let me do it, then I had to teach it to solidify the learning.

From John Maxwell, I learned the Five-Step Equipping Formula, and I'll teach it to you to you here:


## Step 1: I do it.

I call this the "getting good" step. For a leader to build trust, they must have competence. This kind of leadership credibility comes more naturally if you were promoted from an "execution-level" role to a role leading or supervising others who are doing the role you're deeply experienced in.

At times, leaders need to lead beyond their technical experience. When this happens, you still have to become competent through learning. So "get good" in your own execution and understanding, and through learning from others who hold the role.

If you're leading employees in a role you've never held directly, prepare to lead by shadowing experienced employees who hold the role, and cultivating the competence to supervise effectively. Schedule time to work with them and get good at understanding the challenges and keys to effectiveness in that role. If appropriate, participate in the execution of that role alongside the experienced employee.


## Step 2: I do it, and an employee is with me.

This is the teaching step. Imagine you were teaching a teenager to drive. You don't just hand them the keys and say "Drive!" Do you? No! You would sit in the driver's seat and they would sit in the passenger's seat as you showed them all the correct things to do in the car. You would teach them how to stop and go, how to change lanes and use a blinker, how to adjust the mirrors and shift gears. In step two, you are teaching and equipping the employee to be successful. You are developing their potential.

## Step 3: The employee does it, and you are with them.

Ok, we're back to the driving lesson, except this time you are in the passenger's seat. Did you do a good job of teaching? Are you going to scream and yell at them when they make a mistake and create fear? This is the coaching step. You can't reach over and push the gas or the brake, or grab the steering wheel. In this step you are coaching them to utilize the skills you taught them in step two. When they veer off path, try to unlock their success through questions and support them so they can get their own level-one mastery.

## Step 4: They do it.

The employee does it and you aren't hovering over them. You aren't in the passenger seat. You aren't micro-managing them. You give them the keys and let them drive. Establish expectations like you would with that teenager and then let them go. Have check-ins along the way to ensure the learning has stuck and you don't need to do some additional coaching or course-correcting. As you check in from time to time, you gain trust with them and their mastery means they complete the assignments and tasks without you at all.

## Step 5: They do it, and another employee is with them.

This is the succession step. We are now multiplying your team while solidifying your employee's competence through teaching. Not only do you not have to do the tasks anymore, the employee you equipped is building support for a future where they may need help with the tasks. While they are doing this, you can focus on other high-priority responsibilities or you can take another employee through the equipping steps for other tasks and responsibilities you have as the leader.

Equipping doesn't happen overnight. It takes effort. But like a good workout, you become stronger and less fatigued as you deepen the skills and strength of those you lead. Intrinsically motivated employee retention skyrockets when you equip, because they feel valued by you, as well as empowered to become more free and skilled.

Every person, including you, has untapped potential. True leaders unlock that potential in everyone of their employees.

I am who I am today, where I am today, because various leaders reached down and coached me to a new level of potential. Who I am today is not who I was when I left home at eighteen years old. I had zero skill in communicating with, or leading, others. I grew up in a home that was violent, abusive, and lacked any role models for healthy communication and leadership. It was a home that created fear and lacked trust.

I needed mentorship and development. I needed leaders to see my worth and potential and pull it out of me. I am grateful for many along the way who have done this in the many different roles I have been in throughout my career.

At twenty-three, I had a leader challenge me to begin a growth journey. I read my first book that year. Over the last three decades, I have read hundreds of books, listened to hundreds of podcasts, attended many conferences, and been mentored by some of the greatest leaders on the planet, including John C Maxwell and Quint Studer. They are just a couple of the leaders that I've had the honor to sit at the table with, have phone calls with, and learn directly from. I've learned from them to lead from the heart instead of the head. But more importantly, they have been a part of equipping the leader I am today.

Like me, you have employees, and maybe you are one as well, that need development, mentoring, and equipping to be better humans, better leaders, or better employees.

Your job is to grow yourself and then transfer that growth to others by seeing their value and potential, and then get busy developing them to their fullest potential, not just within their job. What is your plan for developing others? Do you know the skills and behaviors you need the team to be really good at?

As the leader, you have to become the chief trainer and quit waiting on Human Resources to do it for you. And quit expecting employees to get better on their own. When we train and develop our team, they will love us and stay with us longer. It is the number one reason an employee chooses to stay or leave.

# Take Action:

This tactic is all about making it possible for each team member to bring their best to work. Wherever you are in your organization, there is something you can do to help others overcome barriers to top performance. Use these examples to imagine more ways to accommodate individual needs, eliminate barriers to helping, and help everyone thrive on the job.

**If You're on the Frontline:**

- Evaluate where you feel friction, or notice barriers that you or a colleague are having to overcome where help from your leaders might reduce burnout or unlock better results. How can you speak up for yourself to request help bringing equity to the workplace for you and those you work with?

- Who on the team seems to have a bad attitude or not be performing as well as others. Can you notice any barriers they have to deal with that others do not? Does seeing the extra effort they have to extend to overcome an inequitable barrier change how you feel about helping or encouraging them when they're overwhelmed?

**If You're a Manager or Supervisor:**

- Use the Strategic Reflection to notice where you may have the opportunity to improve performance and talent retention through equitable accommodations.

- Assess your own mindset. What does fairness mean to you? Can you strengthen your justice paradigm by recognizing the many kinds of benefits that grow when organizations make the effort to bring everyone up to an equitable vantage point?

**If You're an Executive Leader:**

- You are responsible for the lion's share of your company's culture toward equity in the workplace. What are you doing to advance an equitable workplace where the individuals who work there can truly bring their best every day?

- Savvy leaders often find a competitive advantage for their company through overcoming barriers to work. Visionary insight in this area can broaden your talent pool, unlock productivity, and even expand your market reach to customers.

# Retention Tactic #5:
## *Respond to Feedback*

I f you are a leader, you need to give feedback to your team. But that's not what this section is about. Effective leaders don't just communicate to their employees by speaking; they communicate understanding by listening to feedback from team members.

Even in great companies and on teams with positive culture, there will always be things that aren't working as well or as smoothly as they could. And potential for growth and new avenues for success often come through listening to feedback from the team members who do the work every day.

In an average workplace, employees only offer feedback in the form of quitting when they can't endure the problems in the culture any longer. Some organizations have tried without success to solicit input and creative problem solving from staff members. Most often these initiatives fail when leaders either ignore the feedback, make excuses or delay addressing issues, or reject the feedback by blame shifting. Many workers have learned not to respond to requests for input because they have paid in political or reputational currency for past attempts to speak up. For most, the potential negative ramifications of trying to change things aren't worth the unlikely chance anything will come of it.

How's your company doing?

Do your leaders try to listen to employees?

Do a few well-placed individuals have sway on how things work, and other voices aren't ever sought out? Do you have to have a bunch of letters behind your name, years of seniority, or a shiny title before you're allowed to speak up?

One of the most effective ways to keep talent on your team is to create effective pathways for every voice in the organization to be heard. In the "Release" section we'll talk about how to gather insights from employees who are leaving the company. But why wait for people to go before taking their perspective seriously?

It's important to realize that talent retention is only one of the big benefits of having an effective feedback process at work in your organization. Hearing insights from every seat on the bus can improve efficiency, reduce waste, and guide innovation. Using a Talent Lock Conversation, you can spot trends of loss as well as opportunities for profit much earlier if you're listening to a wide range of perspectives. The financial growth that comes from these kinds of ongoing learning conversations throughout the organization are massive, and compound over time.

Imagine catching a strategic flaw in the first quarter it showed up, rather than three quarters deep. How different is the conversation with your clients or stakeholders when you're making an adjustment early, rather than explaining the loss that has accrued? And when it comes to innovation and growth opportunities, it can be hard to calculate the value of missing the trend, or arriving after your competitors have all figured it out.

## Retention in Highly Regulated Industries

Maybe this sounds like a nice tactic for teams that can be highly creative; maybe it's just for businesses whose leadership wants to innovate and is willing to spend money experimenting to catch new trends.

If your organization is highly regulated—either by government regulation or by fierce financial constriction or "best practices" that don't leave room for much experimentation—it can be tempting to skip this tactic.

But this is not for the touchy-feely, nap pod-using tech startups. CEO of CommWell Health, Pamela Tripp used this technique and others like it to take failing hospital systems and turn them into top performers within five years.[20] Even in the rigidly regulated healthcare industry, strong leaders use this technique of soliciting quality feedback from stakeholders at every level in the organization.

When I spoke with L. David Marquette, author of *Turn the Ship Around*, I was amazed to hear the impact of turning order takers into leaders. It's hard to imagine a more highly regulated industry than the military command of a nuclear sub.

Your receptionist has insights into how the company runs that your CFO will never think of; the "tech guy" notices recurring, costly problems that never hit your radar. This extends to each department, and the entire pecking order of staff. Each person on the team has a divergent perspective, and the insights they can give you are gold.

In order to profit from the different perspectives your team members have, you need to learn to ask questions to invite every person on the team to have input on how things work at your organization.

One of the biggest challenges for any organization is engagement and compliance of staff with necessary processes and policies. We need our employees to be fully bought in, ready to do what needs to be done. If they're not on board, they'll end up resisting us or working around the systems we're trying to put in place. Often, changes aren't what staff would want. Whether it's difficult choices about pay and benefits, or shifts in the hours or delivery of services, engaging your staff in the changes that they will have to implement can be the difference between forward progress and years of managed anarchy.

Employee feedback can come in many forms. From anonymous voting to open brainstorming sessions to rewarding individuals for making substantive suggestions. If you can get your employees talking to you about what would make work better, their sense of ownership in strengthening the organization grows.

## Having to say No

Most leaders would like to make their teams happy, but feel that the feedback they'd receive would be impossible to follow through on. "They'll just all want more time off, but we can't give them that." Sometimes leaders will ask me, "What do I do if they all ask for a raise and I have to say no? Won't they feel like we're not listening?"

I feel those leaders' pain. But inevitably, when our team works with theirs, I find that they're asking the wrong questions. When we ask a bunch of burnt-out workers what they need to work longer and harder, they ask for raises and bonuses in part because they know you can't give them. But if we ask questions like "how could onboarding new clients be less exhausting for the intake staff?" or "what are our customer's most draining demands?" we start to get information from our people.

Asking "what would make accomplishing this priority more effortless for your team?" or even "what part of your day do you dread the most, and why?" can help begin to identify pain points that can usually be eliminated without cutting a big check. When you ask the team to brainstorm together to identify possible solutions to the things that are irritating them or slowing down productivity, most leaders are surprised at how manageable the changes often are.

In a worst case scenario, if your staff collaborates to suggest a solution to a serious problem and it's absolutely not something you can give them, communicate authentically with them to convey your value of them, your appreciation of their solution, and a clearer picture of the barrier, then ask them, "how can we work around this barrier to get you more of what you need?"

Seeking to understand rather than thinking you know the answer already means staying in the conversation with your staff when demands seem impossible. If you involve them in the suggested improvements, keep them involved in making their solutions viable. In doing this, your team will have an increased understanding of what the company needs, and a strengthened sense of their place in the company.

## Resolve Small Irritations

We've heard it's the straw that broke the camel's back. As cliché as it is, sometimes the small irritations create more friction, resentment, and burnout within a team than large issues. Some frustrations impact everyone on the team, and others disproportionately affect specific roles. Technical equipment that has frequent errors can waste time consistently, frustrating any team member who relies on it to complete their responsibilities. Outdated forms, never having enough of certain office supplies, red tape that serves no purpose, or other small irritations can take up employee bandwidth better held in reserve to deal with real emergencies, tough client demands, and sprinting toward stretch goals.

What would happen if you asked your direct reports, colleagues, or manager what little thing bugs them and you looked for an easy fix? While some problems are complex, expensive, or difficult to fix, it's shocking how many small irritations can be cleared through curious reflection, and a small action.

## How to Resolve Small Irritations

If you're the boss, solving small problems is a great goal for one of your one-on-one coaching or mentoring sessions with employees. You can be very direct about it, letting each employee know you're trying to deal with some of the little irritations that are bogging the team down and asking them, "can you think of anything that's small but frustrating that maybe I could help eliminate or improve for you?"

Not up for the direct route? Remember where you came from. Were you promoted to leader because of your ability to do the job of the people you now lead? Don't let the move to the leader's office make you forget what things were like in your previous role.

Never done the job of those you're leading now? Go work a day or shadow an employee to deepen your understanding of their daily pressures. Learn what they are doing, their workflows, and frustrations. Get curious, pay extra attention, and discover by observation where you hear voices rising, tension snap, or irritation buzz around you. In group meetings, do team members scuffle to grab one of the comfy office chairs because a couple of the seats are old and stiff? What would it take to get rid of the hated chairs to reduce friction? Is one team member interrupted anytime someone needs replacement supplies that could be divvied out to reduce interruptions for the employee who is currently storing them for the team?

If your leadership role involves customer relationships in any way, turn this tactic toward the customer interactions and discover any small friction that your team experiences from the customer that might be easily solved. Do customer requests come in a difficult form, wasting time because something isn't clearly communicated? Is the way one specialty handles notes complicating care for other departments? Do all clients ask for something outside the scope of what your team does and could a small change in marketing or client onboarding reduce this confusion? The customer isn't always right. We need to spend time with customers and listen to our staff to determine the training needed for our team or the support needed with difficult conversations they are having.

If you're not the boss but you have even one person collaborating with or working under you, then see what you can do to reduce friction or irritation for that person! You might be shocked how this improves the energy and engagement of your colleagues.

If you're only in charge of yourself, you may still be able to reduce something irritating or draining in the environment. Even just becoming aware of what is causing you friction can help you redirect your own process or have insight about what you need in order for things to improve.

At the end of the day, resolving irritations in the workplace always requires some flexibility, creativity, or bravery. Irritations stick around because routines and patterns are hard to change. Problems arise even when managers and workers have the best intentions. And sometimes speaking up to ask for things to be made better can feel like it "costs you" in office politics or reputation. Instead of forcing people around you to suffer or spend their professional relationship currency asking for changes, do what you can to reduce irritation without being asked.

Sometimes irritations come in the form of workplace gossip, poor manners, or unaddressed communication problems on the team. Patterns of sarcasm, exaggeration, and cliques of popularity can leave a bad taste in the mouth of hardworking employees. Though not "big enough" for them to waste relationship capital trying to get them dealt with, they can be like a pebble in their shoes that prevents an employee from running at top speeds. Dealing with these distractions in the environment will help you retain the good employees you don't want to lose. It can also help mediocre employees switch off autopilot and have energy to bring more of their best to the job.

## Everyone Must Pull Their Weight

Maybe you're like the self-motivated, high-achieving leaders I work with all the time who don't love the idea of "spoon feeding" or coddling employees. It's important to set meaningful expectations of excellence and both challenge and assist our teams in reaching them.

As an individual achiever, our focus should always be on bringing our best, diverting our energy from complaining about irritations. We want to be someone who steps over roadblocks, rather than sitting around waiting for things to get fixed. But as a leader, it's important to understand the opportunity inside irritations and workplace friction. Friction slows everyone down. Irritations—especially the petty, small stuff—represent some of the easiest ways for you to boost the speed and agility of your colleagues and employees.

If you find yourself thinking "I wouldn't let that bother me," your personality is showing. As a leader, be the person who makes a habit of pulling the rocks out of all your runners' shoes. It's amazing how the energy in a team culture can shift into high gear when employees start to feel like their leaders care and work to eliminate the barriers to their flow.

## Listen Early

As a leader, it's important to address small irritations for your employees before they become bigger problems that can negatively impact productivity and morale. Here are some ways you can resolve small irritations for your employees:

### 1. Listen actively

When an employee brings up a small irritation, listen actively to what they have to say. Make sure you understand the issue and ask clarifying questions if necessary. This shows that you value their input and take their concerns seriously. Don't be the leader who avoids all irritations. They will only get bigger if you aren't willing to engage and redirect employee focus. Make sure you are listening to understand versus respond.

### 2. Offer solutions

Once you understand the issue, offer potential solutions that could help alleviate the irritation. Ask the employee for their input on these solutions and work together to find one that works best. Ask them what they have tried already or in the past that worked in a similar situation. Your goal should be to get their focus on a positive solution instead of leaving them in a negative, complaining, and maybe even gossipy state of behavior.

### 3. Follow through

After agreeing on a solution, make sure to follow through with any action items assigned to yourself or others involved in resolving the issue. This demonstrates your commitment to addressing employee concerns and builds trust between you and your team. Gain a commitment from them to do what they said they would and then report back to you.

### 4. Show appreciation

Finally, show appreciation for your employees' patience and willingness to bring up small irritations before they become bigger problems. A simple acknowledgement can go a long way in improving morale.

By taking these steps, leaders can effectively resolve small irritations for their employees and create a positive work environment where everyone feels heard and valued.

# Take Action:

This tactic is all about responding to feedback from every team member. Wherever you are in your organization, there is something you can do to reduce friction and increase the ease of working together or serving your customers. Here are some action steps as examples. Use them as a springboard to imagine more ways to let insights flow into action so your team gets stronger and more energized for high performance.

**If You're on the Frontline:**
- Pay attention to where friction is showing up in processes or small irritations are eating your bandwidth. Collaborate with a colleague or leader and use your insights to make work better.

- When things aren't working, or you notice a major problem at work, don't assume everyone else knows what the problem is and just isn't dealing with it. Sometimes you have useful insights that need to be passed on. Develop your communication skills to get strong at speaking up and become part of the solution in your workplace when the stakes are high. Don't speak only with your resignation.

**If You're a Manager or Supervisor:**

- Use one-on-one coaching and team meetings as opportunities to learn from your team about what isn't working. If you don't want negativity to dominate your meetings, chances are people feel resistance to voicing negative opinions. Create a positive space for constructive, negative feedback by inviting people to share insights where friction or process failure seems to be happening.

- Ask yourself what feedback you've been getting and ignoring. If you're not sure, ask a few employees what the most irritating problem that never seems to get solved is. Get curious about why you are dismissing it. Do you feel powerless to make changes because of your industry? Afraid to let people speak up if they will ask for something you'll have to say no to? Stop hiding from feedback and use this strategy to engage.

**If You're an Executive Leader:**

- What processes and expectations have you set in place for managers and leaders to be learning from staff? Is yours a culture where everyone is "too busy" to actually listen to the voices on their team? Take ownership of this problem and make room for feedback to flow in your organization.

- Only a leader can shift the trend of people being punished for giving unpopular feedback. Take an honest look at the voices being ignored or canceled in your workplace; disregarding people as negative is lazy leadership. Seek to learn from these voices and make it safe for employees to share unpopular feedback.

## Extended Resources

Embed feedback questions inside your company using tools like the S.T.A.Y. Onboarding, one-on-one coaching, and SOAR Team Meeting agendas. Come borrow some of the tools working for teams in every industry at **HarbourResources.com**.

# Release: Have Them Sing Your Praises

No matter how amazing your company is, you will lose people. Even the best team cultures have turnover. But most of us sort our exiting employees into "don't go!" or "good riddance!" piles. We don't latch onto the opportunities for their exit to become a productive part of the culture of the company.

Maybe your company is losing workers right now. If so, you're not alone. Many companies are just trying to survive the talent loss, and begin the arduous process of finding new recruits. But any employee exit from your company offers unique opportunities and information that could turn the tables for your company moving forward. We must always remember that the best recruiting tactic is the retention of the employees you already have on your team. So, when you lose someone, you need to learn as much as you can from the loss.

Quality offboarding has the potential to close the loop of your team's growth cycle, amplifying gains and strengthening insights for the future.

Whatever the reason for an employee's departure, there are things they can teach you about how to improve the strength of your company culture. They can also participate in supporting the person who will take over the role they are vacating. They can even yield secrets for success in hiring and training their replacement.

Whether you're actively losing people right now, or holding steady, getting these strategies in place will keep you from losing the great value hiding in the next employee who walks out the door.

In the beginning of this book I discussed *sapere vedere*. Do you remember? Turn the process of hindsight, foresight, and insight toward the release process so you can make wise changes. Otherwise, you will be stuck assuming turnover is just part of leadership. I'm saying you will never lose anyone if you follow all the advice in this book, but you can prevent more than is necessary.

In hindsight, asking your leaving employees to help you understand their role better, the challenges they faced, and the support needed to make it better for the next person in the role will help you make the necessary leadershifts. Using foresight gives you the chance to upskill, or even shift, the role by asking yourself questions like, "what type of person do I need in this role next?" Use your insight from these two conversations to make stronger hiring choices in the future, and be ready to equip and activate the potential of that new person when they arrive.

# Release Tactic #1:
## *Gather Exit Insights*

We organized this book to begin by helping you retain and develop the employees you already have because that is the highest return on effort you can have as a leader. Energizing and repairing what isn't working well in your current team workflow pays the highest dividends with less unsecured risk. But immediately after addressing your current workers, we turn to focus on the "Release" phase of your talent life cycle. It's the most overlooked portion of the talent lifecycle, and yet this step can be used to drastically improve your long-term turnover and team morale.

If your current organization is like most companies, the minute you suspect that an employee is on their way out, you will be tempted to cut your losses, minimize investment, and shift all your energy away from them and toward the search for a replacement. Whether we're glad to see them go, or overwhelmed at the prospect of redistributing their workload, we fail to recognize we desperately need the insights that could be gained from this worker who is leaving.

Because we don't expect to find insights from employees who quit or have to be let go, we are also at risk of losing talent that could have been kept. We would like to think that if the person could have been saved by correction, support, or repositioning that it would have happened already. But sometimes this gets missed.

Take a step beyond avoiding this one instance of turnover and you'll see that every ex-employee becomes an ambassador for what it's like to work at your company. Think about it: they leave you and re-enter the pool of talent candidates filled with their ideas and dissatisfaction and insights about why they couldn't work at your company. Whether you dismiss an employee or not, they still will have an impact on your employment brand. Jumping straight to recruiting a replacement without making any investment to offboard them well is like failing to repair gashes in your ship's hull and just screaming for more people to come bail water.

Additionally, sometimes the information you need to learn from the employee who is leaving isn't about keeping them or making them happy; sometimes you just need to take effective steps to download some of the specialized knowledge and insights the employee has gained during their tenure to transfer that to their replacement when they arrive. We call this "enriching the onboarding process through offboarding." Let's start there with one of the clear ways most companies can benefit from effective exit interviews.

## Notice How Roles have Shifted

Chances are that if a team member is with you for any significant period of time, the scope of their responsibilities will shift and grow over time. Regardless of the job description that person was hired for, they now meet a list of implicit and explicit expectations on a daily, weekly, monthly, and annual basis. Sometimes we don't have any clue how much has migrated onto one team member's plate until it comes time to replace that person.

One significant part of the offboarding process that I teach my consulting clients involves instructing employees who give notice to begin immediately developing a twelve-week self-replacement plan to train the next person to be hired. An important piece of that task includes clearly delineating every responsibility they have, and what jobs they're doing.

Sometimes what becomes clear in this process is that replacing this employee may mean bringing in more than one replacement. Simply hiring someone based on that person's initial job description would mean expecting a new recruit to take on an evolved workload without all the years their predecessor put in to manage everything. It may also mean a redistribution of tasks or responsibilities in order to balance and optimize workflow on the team moving forward.

"I'm doing like, six jobs around here," says an exhausted employee. We may dismiss them as complainers, but what if they're right? What if they are doing parts of six different jobs? Whatever the reason for an employee's departure—whether they leave on good terms or not—be prepared to get someone else to do all of what they had been doing...or brace yourself for things to be missed.

## How to Have Dynamic Exit Interviews

One of the ways to let exiting team members enrich the onboarding process is asking them to participate in developing a twelve-week plan to train their replacement. But even if this isn't part of your culture yet, simple exit questions can reveal a lot of valuable information that can be used to strengthen your onboarding process for the future.

**Ask questions like:**

- What was the most confusing part of your job when you started? If you were to explain it to your younger self so it was less confusing, how would you teach it?

- When did you finally feel solid on your core skills, and what got you there? In hindsight, is there something you think we could have done to get you to that solid feeling sooner?

- What do you wish you knew when you first started?

- What were your keys to success on effective days here?

If you look closely, these questions apply to any job, at every level of the workplace food chain. Whether you're offboarding frontline personnel, managers, or administrative staff, asking these questions will provide information that can be woven into your onboarding process for future hires.

Take the impact a step further when you onboard your next hire using the insights of past employees. By giving credit to previous employees who've added their insights, you foster a culture of recognition. When recruits hear that this onboarding training is built not just by managers, but is sourced from the insights of others who have been in their seat, colleagues and predecessors, onboarding is often seen in a new light.

This provides a great opportunity to set the expectation for new recruits that whenever they leave their role or the company, they too will be asked to contribute wisdom and insights to help others make a strong start at the company. Teams that employ this full-circle mentality with onboarding and offboarding close the loop on lost energy and the "brain drain" of constantly "starting over."

Leaders: this is another great time to implement foresight and do some future casting with the exiting employee to create a better role for their replacement, and if you're lucky enough you might be able to influence them to stay in the process.

## Reflect on Growth & Meaning

One big piece of offboarding is building a culture of meaning. We do this when a team knows we're not just robots moving widgets; there's something meaningful each person contributes to with their work each day.

When we offboard people with meaning, we honor the meaning of the work done by the employee, and the growth they experienced and created for the company. Even though they're leaving, the meaning they generated is worth honoring. When we engage our teams in a culture of meaning, it helps protect them against the worst effects of stress and change in the workplace, and reduces their vulnerability to burnout. Meaning comes from noticing the value that you are creating or experiencing in the world.

Meaning is often found from paying attention to our responses to pressure, our resilience to setbacks, and our connectedness to those around us. The best form of gratitude honors a person for the meaning they contributed in the workplace, thanking them for bringing that to the company.

If we look closely enough when a team member leaves, their departure may be due to the unavoidable fact that they've outgrown their role. Whether they've become skilled enough to do more than their current role will allow them, or they've grown in different interests or priorities, if you take the opportunity to notice and honor their growth, you will set a positive tone for their offboarding, rather than allowing for a hostile vibe to dominate.

Reflect back to the Mother Teresa quote I shared at the beginning of this section. You are creating a ripple effect into the future; is it the one you want to create? Is the ripple a tsunami of destruction or a wave of inspiration to challenge your employees to be more than they even believe is possible?

Even if the person didn't "outgrow" their job, connecting to and honoring the value created by them at the company shifts the impact their departure leaves on the team.

One way to facilitate this is to include questions in the exit interview that allow the employee to reflect on and share the meaning they experienced while at your company. Questions could include ones such as:

- What's been the best part of doing this job?

- How did you grow while you were here?

- What are you most proud of yourself for from your time here?

- Where did you surprise yourself with what you were capable of?

- How would you wish you were remembered when you've moved on?

You might be surprised at the answers you get. And if you attempt some of these questions and encounter resistance, that may be a sign that your employees are not used to looking for meaning. If you thank them for their contribution—and use specific descriptions of what value you saw them create while at the company—and they react badly, that's a serious red flag. It may mean that yours isn't a culture of meaning and gratitude yet. It may be that with some changes in your company culture, you would not have lost this team member.

As you hear their answers to these questions, you're learning insights that can be used to inspire and paint a picture for the replacement that will come. Take notes, and remember that sharing these positive insights during onboarding can help the new hire benefit from this employee's exit in a unique way.

When utilizing this strategy remember *sapere vedere*. This is your shot to learn, grow, and change as a leader. When I started my own business in 2006, I hired some team members that didn't work out for various reasons. Some were because of my leadership. Some were because I didn't have a good S.T.A.Y. process in place. Some were because I blamed the employees and didn't learn what I could do better.

You may hear some things you do not like in the release conversations. You may even hear some things that aren't your fault and you could blame your leader or corporate office for, but resist the urge to blame shift or get defensive. In this strategy you must stay in a posture of learning so you can effect change in the future and create a ripple of positive growth.

# Take Action:

This tactic is all about collecting insights from employees who are leaving your company. Wherever you are in your organization, there is something you can do to contribute to the knowledge and meaning of your role, and leave the team better than you found them. Here are some action steps as examples. Use them as a springboard to imagine more ways to learn as much as you can from every person who leaves.

**If You're on the Frontline:**

- Whenever possible, learn from others who have been in your role. Whether they help out with it from time to time or used to be "you" for the organization, get their input to make you smarter as you engage your workload going forward.

- Offload the stress and anxiety that you experience when someone leaves your team by identifying and expressing gratitude for the meaningful way that person helped the team or served the mission while they were there. This can be especially necessary if there is a negative undertone to the person's departure. Connect to the meaning of their role (and your own) to reduce the negative impacts on your ability to engage.

**If You're a Manager or Supervisor:**

- Make an effort to learn from the employees who are leaving. Institute thorough exit interviews if you have the power to do so. If not, do your own exit interview and draw the employee who is leaving into the process of preparing for their replacement. Make sure you acquire a full picture of the ways their role changed or expanded while they held it so your new hire can be more effectively chosen.

- Go beyond "why are you leaving" questions and see what else the employees who are leaving can teach you about the role they held, interdepartmental dynamics, your competing employers' offerings, customer service, or satisfaction insights, and more.

**If You're an Executive Leader:**

- Audit your organization's exit interview process. If you have turnover above 5% for the last year, outsource or expand your offboarding process to learn more about what is costing your company employees.

- Some companies roll out layoffs or fire employees so quickly their teams are left shocked as well as thrown into transition. In tactic 4 you'll learn more about discussing transitions. But at this point, ask yourself if your company's processes even allow enough time for mining exit insights. If the answer is no, change the offboarding window to stop losing insights from this portion of the talent life cycle.

# Release Tactic #2:
## *Address Bullies & Barriers*

None of us want to have unfair workplaces, and I haven't met a leader yet who propped up a bully in the workplace on purpose.

And yet both happen anyway.

According to Thomas Dahlborg, "The impact of bullying is great. Not just to teamness and employee engagement and satisfaction, which in and of themselves are incredibly important, but also specific to healthcare, this is about harm and harming. Harming one another and harming our patients and families. We can and we must do better—together."

There are dozens of reasons that problems in workplace equality or toxic communication patterns can escape our notice as leaders. Every leader needs to build in fail-safes to help them recognize when something is wrong in the culture, especially if it's flying under the top leader's radar.

One of those fail-safes is to listen openly to employees who have decided to leave. It's tempting to dismiss the negative feedback of exiting employees and ignore their input. We falsely assume that because they're "not bought in" their feedback won't have validity. However, an exiting employee may have information that you as the leader desperately need to hear. What you must know is the number one reason for departures in all industries is an underlying lack of belief in leadership and often a frustration with team dynamics. You are the leader of the team, so you will be blamed when you don't do the hard work of leadership and dealing with bullies and barriers.

Exit interviews are a key part of this. That's why Tactic #1 is Gather Exit Insights. By asking the right questions of employees who give notice, we can sometimes discover problems in the culture that need remedy. Sometimes by choosing to care about the employee who has felt written off, we earn the employee's trust back. If we fix the flaws in the workplace, we will be saved from losing more people in the future. We may even end up retaining the employee we were about to lose.

If you see the exiting employee as a unique ally, you will listen to their complaints without defensiveness. Take the opportunity to learn something about your company that perhaps no one else is able to tell you.

And once you've listened you need to do something about it.

## Take Charge

Between you and me, I know a lot of strong, well-intentioned managers and top-level leaders who have been tempted to sweep the complaints of ex-employees under the rug because they don't want to give their company a black eye. They hope that they can just give some positive nudges, or a few more training hours to their managers, but still not directly address the problems that angry ex-employees pointed at.

But sometimes we can't just add in more positive training; sometimes we have to take action to dismantle a toxic process, fire a tyrannical employee who doesn't respond to correction, or enforce policies to bring higher equity to the workplace.

If you feel like the demand for workplace equity is just some new extension of "political correctness," let's pause for a second. As leaders or managers, we often have a bias toward seeing success and failure in our own image. We take ownership for our efforts, discipline, and character, and assume that the same processes of opportunity and success are available to others who are willing to do what we have done.

Every human alive is influenced by how they grew up. Like a fish in our own personal seas, we don't know how greatly our own perspective is influencing us, because we live inside of it.

When it comes to dealing with inequity in the workplace, it can help to take a perspective check and use an insightful framework such as those crafted by Kim Scott and her team at Radical Candor. Look for bias, prejudice, bullying, discrimination, harassment, and physical violations as different threads of inequity that show up in veiled ways in even well-meaning workplaces.

Quantifying the bias in your perspective, or the bias represented in your workplace practices is not a blame-throwing, shame game. It's a tactical process used to engage and deepen the vitality of your company culture through decisive choice.

In the words of Kim Scott:

"It would be nice to think you can avoid hiring bullies. Unfortunately, bullying is a behavior, not a personality type; while some people are more prone to it, we all engage in it from time to time for the simple reason that it can be an effective way to establish or maintain status or to coerce others. And bullying will continue until you, as a leader, make it clear that it simply won't work in your organization."[24]

You catch that? Bullying is a behavior. Like theft, or lateness, or swearing at customers, the behavior can flourish with permission or be smothered with consequences. Consequences aren't about creating an emotional shame around a behavior; they're a way of making undesirable behaviors be seen to backfire on the person who uses them.

# Three Levels of Consequences for Negative Behaviors

While this structure of levels for consequences can be used to discourage any number of behaviors on your team, it's important to note that bullying deserves the same approach.

## Level 1: Negative Feedback

Whether it's a brief private conversation after a meeting, or a formal coaching session with a clear and documented reprimand, negative feedback is the first step. Often bosses and managers don't effectively engage this because they hope the behavior will go away on its own. Not to mention, even leaders and managers are human; and many of us mortals hate confrontation. In worse scenarios, I watch leaders who see negative behavior silently begin to gather validations they can use to fire an employee rather than leading the employee to improve.

If you have done the work from the values section of this book, these difficult conversations should be wrapped around alignment of your values. In our coaching at Harbour Resources, we help leaders create their values and then point them toward conversations about the behavior alignment or misalignment versus making personal attacks against an employee. It is much easier to share with an employee how their behavior fails to align with company values and behavior expectations versus saying "you can't act that way anymore." People have a tendency to go where we point them. So while you need to be clear about which behaviors don't align with the values in order to prompt clear change, the values provide a positive target to aim for.

Done in a private, uninflammatory way, giving unambiguous pushback on bullying behavior sends a signal that their behavior is backfiring. Combine this with clarity about the consequences if the behavior continues. In these conversations you must do two things: gain agreement on the desired behavior change, and commit to accountability through consequences. Consequences may be prescribed by your company already; ask for agreement that they understand what the consequences are if the behavior is repeated. In some cases, you can invite the employee to collaborate with you in agreeing on the feedback process, asking "if you miss the mark on our agreement, how should I handle this and hold you accountable?" This should not be an abusive conversation, but part of its value is that it doesn't feel good. It is okay if you can't find a comfortable way to confront behaviors that violate your company's values. Being willing to work through this with an employee shows you value them because you are helping them know what will cost them if they don't change.

## Level 2: Essential Consequences

One of the ways to provide consequences for bullying or other inequitable behaviors in the workplace is to make repeated behavior disqualify that team member from incentives, rewards, bonuses, and other essential rewards at work. As a leader, how can you bake fairness and culture-preserving consequences into your reward structure? Be sure of this: if negative feedback is ignored, and team members continue to use bullying behaviors to come out on top in the essential rewards of the workplace, that bullying behavior is being rewarded.

As my mentor Quint Studer once said, "What we permit, we promote."

Let's make sure I said that clearly. If bullies keep winning in your workplace, you are rewarding bullying. Don't pass the buck and pretend "it's just a tough world." Every workplace is created by the members and leaders who are part of it. If the reward structure needs to change to provide essential consequences for unfair or destructive behavior, then work to change it.

I recommend starting with behavior goals that move people in a positive direction. If they miss the mark, the lost reward must be desirable enough that it will hopefully create change. I coach my clients to start with small increments of unpaid days off. A day or two without pay from the work schedule can escalate in obvious repercussions. Being disqualified from team perks for a specific period of time, or other major motivators show the employee you are serious about them complying with the cultural values they are violating. If these motivations are inadequate, you may need to step up and fire them.

I am a believer in coaching people up, but when this doesn't work, we must coach them out.


## Level 3: Global Consequences

If you are not willing to fire employees who bully, even essential consequences may not be enough to drive the toxic behavior out of the office. Listen to the employees leaving your company. Are people moving up the ranks of promotion, climbing the ladder on the backs of those they're bullying? Stop promoting them, or you will never stem the tide of fleeing talent. There are a lot of ways we reward behavior at work. Attention in meetings and career advancement. Short of losing their job, loss of power and influence can provide the necessary global consequences so you interrupt the flourishing of bullying behavior in your culture.


# Provide Accountability to Low Performers

If you haven't managed to identify inequitable work distribution while it's happening, the loss of a strong employee can be the wakeup call. Because of this, sometimes the action that needs to be taken during release of one employee is accountability towards low performers still remaining on the team.

Worker shortages mean the strongest staff members are often overwhelmed with extra work. This amplifies when a team member is lost. This alone can be too much for an employee to sustain long term. But in my experience it becomes untenable when employees are forced to pick up slack from a low performer who isn't making the effort to improve. Any person who is "not pulling their weight" inflates burnout for everyone else.

As a supervisor, it can be tempting to overlook imbalances between workers' workloads. If one of our rockstars ends up filling in the gaps for the weaker players, we can falsely label that as "teamwork" and even praise them for it. But as a leader, we need to concern ourselves with addressing the holes in the weak performer's skills and engagement.

When low performers aren't getting the help they need to improve their skills, they create a perpetual and unnecessary drain on the high performers. This effect may be one of the motivating factors whenever a strong team member decides to leave your company.

If the weakest performers don't get stronger, your strong ones will say things like:

- "If I wasn't doing most of his work along with mine, I'd be okay."

- "I'm so tired of doing all of my work and then half of hers too!"

- "I showed that team how to do it themselves, but they still ask me to do it every month. It feels like they think my time is less valuable than theirs."

Rescue your high performers from carrying weight created by low performers.

This seems obvious, so why don't we deal with it? Often leaders assume that a low performer is just that—a low performer. Instead, they're often a high performer who lacks the skills and development necessary to be effective. Whether they need reskilling, more thorough training, or real-time mentoring and coaching to help them improve, giving them the right kind of feedback can not only improve their performance, but help you retain the high performers they're excessively leaning on.

This may be a time to reflect back to your S.T.A.Y. process. Where did you skip some steps in achieving mastery or the "you"-focused training? Did you expect them to know it already, or did you treat them like a tenured employee because they had experience elsewhere?

Like John Maxwell teaches in his Law of the Chain, "A team is only as strong as its weakest link." Find these weak links or your chain will keep unraveling.

## Pay the Right Kind of Attention to Low Performers

"What am I supposed to do, hold their hand?"

I hear this all the time when I encourage leaders with struggling teams to begin coaching their team consistently. Our perspective is, "I'm a leader, not a daycare manager. Either they need to do the work, or make room for someone who can."

But even self-starters crumple under the pressure of inadequate training, foggy goals, and erratic bursts of direction from the C-Suite. The key is to pay the right kind of attention to low performers so that their weaknesses and mistakes are resolved effectively.

In most workplaces however, the only real attention an employee gets is an annual performance review, in which they're told some things they can improve, a lip service "but you're doing a nice job with this" and given a "cost of living increase based on your performance rating." As if that makes sense.

But when asked what could have been done to get five stars instead of a four and a half, the manager says something vague. Or worse, "nothing, you're doing great here!" After which the employee leaves feeling undervalued. The performance review after all didn't really seem to have much to do with their performance.

Coaching and mentoring your low performers look much different than this. Pair accountability processes with personal development and growth mentoring. Inside a coaching relationship you will gain insight into the employee's barriers and deficits and be able to plan what kind of help and goals are needed to get the low performer back on track.

Can you use *sapere vedere* to make improvements in this tactic? Where has bullying by low workplace performers been an issue for you in the past? What did you say you would do about it when you were the leader? Using your skill of foresight, what do you want the culture of your team to feel like, and be like twelve months from now? Are there any underlying bullying challenges right now? Do you know? What are you doing to make sure your workplace culture is moving you closer to your goal of equity and belonging for all on the team?

In my thirty years of professional leadership experience, communication challenges, performance issues, and stealth bullying are the biggest problems leaders face. It's not the budget or schedule or the myriad of other things we tend to blame. Fix the three things above and ninety percent of your leadership gets easier. Every team deserves a leader who will address these challenges and raise the performance for all team members. Will you be that leader?

Depending on your personality, confrontation needed for these steps can be daunting. Even those with a personality strength for this may find it is easy to do, but far from enjoyable. However, I am wired for these things. I am a High-D on the DISC, a Challenger on the Enneagram. My values are purpose, excellence, and action. I feel compelled to not let anyone get bullied on any team. I see it far too often and do my best to coach others on how to step in and step up.

If you are a leader who struggles in these areas of conversation, you must get a mentor or coach who can help you or you will fail as a leader. I had to get a coach to help me temper my style of leadership and not become the bully to the bully. Build your self-awareness so you can help your organization grow in the right direction.


## Take Action:

This tactic is all about dealing with bullies who are barriers to talent flow in your company. Wherever you are in your organization, there is something you can do to move toward your values and contribute to the right kinds of consequences for bullying. Here are some action steps as examples. Use them as a springboard to imagine more ways to address these problems, so good employees are safe to stay and give their best to the team.

**If You're on the Frontline:**

- If you are burning out because someone on your team is inadequately trained or struggling with their workload, find an effective way to speak up before you wear yourself out. If you are the one who is drowning because your workload is bulging with tasks you don't feel confidently able to handle, ask for support, training, or help. Don't become part of the unnecessary turnover rate.

- If you notice something in the culture that clearly violates the company values, rewarding behaviors the organization says they don't want to see, look for ways to discuss it with the right mentor or leader. Perhaps use the language of values to ask how you can serve the values without being derailed by the contrary element of the work environment. This may lead to your leaders addressing the inconsistency in the culture, or at least give you some help embodying the company values in spite of it.

**If You're a Manager or Supervisor:**

- Get honest with yourself if your personality or conflict avoidance has led you to not give enough accountability and consequences to the low performers and bullies on your team. How can you grow in this area so your whole team doesn't suffer?

- If "what we permit we promote," ask where you are promoting bullying by simply permitting it. Make it safe for employees to raise flags on bullying behavior—when they're leaving or hopefully before.

**If You're an Executive Leader:**

- Only top leadership can make strategic decisions about what kind of essential and global consequences are being given to bullies in the organization. Without an adequate consequence structure, your managers and employees have no protection from bullying. You will lose the talent you need unless you provide this consequence structure. Take the time now to evaluate what's in place and bring it up to par so it can enforce your values throughout the company.

- Check your own behavior. Has bullying worked for you in the past and become part of your leadership style? Sometimes we need an outside perspective on our own leadership. Where can you get help assessing your own performance in this area?

# Release Tactic #3:
## *Rehire & Reposition for Growth*

I f you successfully mine for insights, and address the bullies and barriers that have caused an employee to leave, you may have an opportunity to rehire or reposition that employee in your organization. Research has revealed that it takes longer (often years) for an external hire to perform as well as an internal hire.[26] If you have the chance to reposition someone rather than losing them, the advantages make it worth pursuing.

Sometimes we are unmotivated to do the "extra work" of repositioning someone in our company. Especially if the employee is unhappy (or we're unhappy with them), we don't even consider trying to keep them in the company by changing their role or developing them in some way. One thing that wakes us up to thinking about this is when we take a look at what losing an employee really costs our company.

Do you know the actual cost of turnover on your team? Part of being a leader is thinking like a CEO or business owner and knowing the cost of business and loss. If you think like the CEO of your team, company, or department you must know this number or you will not have the clarity to see which efforts are worth making to fix it. For years as a business owner I didn't know the real cost of my taxes and I would get to the end of a year and not have enough money to cover the bill to Uncle Sam. I would blame others for not doing their job to pay my taxes, yet it was my problem to solve. When I started operating like a CEO I began to put systems in place to fix the problems. You must do the same thing if you want different results from your leadership.

Too often the people who are walking out the door aren't leaving because they can't give us what we need; they're leaving because they don't want to remain in a broken culture, or keep banging their heads against barriers to growth anymore.

Really effective offboarding sometimes ends in a rehire. This happens more often than you might think.

Imagine, if the employee you're most likely to lose right now just needed something. Whether it's to be listened to, to get some of the right kind of help, to gain a skill that would stop them from drowning, or perhaps to become reconnected to the meaning of working at your organization. Maybe they need other team members to improve their performance, but haven't been able to get their needs noticed.

What if they didn't have to leave? What if you didn't have to manage their workload while you looked for a replacement? What if you didn't have to sort through hundreds of résumés, and spend hours in interviews? What if you didn't have to spend weeks doing that and then still have to train someone new to takeover?

Wouldn't it be worth a small investment in the offboarding process to possibly retain a valuable employee? Or better yet, using a Talent Lock Conversation to stop an employee from leaving and ever getting to the release conversation?

Let's pause here and think about *sapere vedere* for a moment. What hindsight could you gain from the conversation we have discussed? What about foresight about the change you could effect for the future? Use the insight from these two questions to strategically move forward on your Quit Losing Talent framework and create the ripple of change in your team.

## Become Mobile Minded

An effective offboarding can reveal that an employee is in the wrong role. Moving them within the company to be more fulfilled and effective can reduce talent loss, and strengthen your team in a different way. How good is your company at recognizing the readiness of your team members for growth and role evolution?

In my over twelve years of formal coaching experience, most leaders I've met just think about the day right in front of them, or the immediate task at hand. Is this the right way to grow, lead and develop people?

Developing requires time, scheduling, and planning. If we don't make this a priority in our leadership, employees either get disengaged or they go elsewhere.

Maybe you aren't in a leadership role; you are an employee and want to grow. Maybe you have to change companies to find that next growth opportunity. But before you go, what would happen if you sought the path for upward mobility where you're at? You would create more value for your company since they wouldn't lose your talent and skills, and you would start out your next "new job" with a world of knowledge about your "new company" already.

If it's easier for an outsider to get into your organization than it is for one of your current employees to seek better opportunities or find a better fit within the company, you have a mobility problem. Often the burnout and low job satisfaction scores of your team members come because the box they've been locked into in your company has stifled their growth.

Your reputation has a ripple effect. Sometimes the rehiring doesn't happen instantaneously. Employees who leave on a good note are more likely to return in the months and years to come. Some will even leave companies, acquire new skills and experience with competitors, and then return stronger and more insightful, and add a whole new level of value to our company and their team. This will only happen if your ripple effect in their life was positive and didn't leave them feeling undervalued.

Think about it this way: if an employee is leaving you anyway, what do you have to lose? Put a small investment of strategy and care into your employee's offboarding process and you will smooth the way for new recruits, reduce the stress of remaining team members, and leave doors open for your investment in this employee to keep bearing fruit even though they're leaving. If you're lucky they may even tell employees at their new company what a great leader you are, and become an unpaid recruiter for you!

# Reposition Roles for Future Growth

Sometimes, even with a solid exit interview, and decisive action to correct barriers that caused someone to leave, you will still lose the employee that you wish you could have kept.

Wise leaders practice *sapere vedere* and look beyond who vacated the chair to ask if the way the role is structured is putting a cap on the potential of the person who sits in this seat. Now is a good time to check to see if the demands and opportunities offered to the person in this role really honor the strengths of the kind of person who comes into it.

Does the role require the high-energy and self-directing initiative of a driven person, but put frustrating limits on their creative freedom? Does it require continuously expanding knowledge—but doesn't give them time within their job to keep learning? Are they forced to compete with colleagues when their productivity would be better with solid collaboration pathways?

Sometimes the very way we have structured someone's job means that we will keep burning out the exact kind of person we need in that role. Whether the person you're losing from the position is willing to let you try to improve things or not, a smart leader will investigate what innovation is needed to let future employees remain engaged with room to grow.

Take a look at your company's mobility statistics. How often do employees make lateral and vertical moves within the organization? If your team has embraced the trend of constantly bringing in external hires, and never repositioning or rarely promoting from within, you've got a golden opportunity to improve your talent retention and development process.

Before we move forward in the release tactics, take time to reflect on how you're doing as a leader. Are you losing the opportunity to learn from a leaving employee because your ego is bruised, saying "everyone leaves eventually" or "they weren't committed to us anyway."

I hear these things a lot from leaders I've worked with in the past, but I rarely hear a leader say "I stepped in and asked some questions I was afraid to ask and was able to change some things and the employee decided to stay and I didn't have to pay another dime to do it." Releasing well is a gold mine right in front of you if you will utilize the ideas shared in this book.

Do you really want to keep dealing with the headaches of turnover, recruitment, and onboarding or hearing your current employees complain about being short staffed when someone leaves? Apply this tactic the next time you get the chance and see the difference—you may be three feet from gold and save the employee.

## Take Action:

This tactic is all about catching the employee headed out the door (or paving the way for them to return again). Wherever you are in your organization, there is something you can do to help talent stick around. Here are some action steps as examples. Use them as a springboard to imagine more ways to encourage potential to grow at your company.

**If You're on the Frontline:**
- Next time you think about changing jobs, get curious about possibilities to grow or move within your current organization. Keep pushing to fulfill your potential where you're at; don't just quietly leave and start over if an internal opportunity might advance you.

- Take advantage of training and mentoring opportunities, or seek them out so that you keep expanding your skills and competencies. Whether you grow at this organization or move to the next one, growth is key for becoming an employee managers will work to retain.

**If You're a Manager or Supervisor:**
- Make an honest list of employees you have mentally labeled as "poor performers" and look at their personality and strengths. Try to step away from seeing them one dimensionally, and ask if they might fulfill their potential and bring more value to the organization in                        another                        role.

Repeat the process with your highly productive employees. Are they burning out where they're at? Sometimes we ignore this if the high performer is carrying a critical role, but look down the road. That employee will burn out eventually. Look for ways to use internal mobility or adjustment of responsibilities to avoid having to release these employees if you can help it.

- Spend a few minutes reflecting on the very real potential of rehiring employees months or years from now. What would have to change about the way employees leave your company now to turn your past employee pool into potential new recruits in the future?

**If You're an Executive Leader:**

- How hard is it for employees to advance within your company? What needs to happen to open up talent development and repositioning opportunities within your company to get the employees you have now in the position where they create the most value? Do employees actually have to go to a new company for the pay increase they need to keep pace with the job market? Do business with these drivers of talent retention.

- Have you set the vision for an employment brand that involves goodwill and strong reputation with ex-employees? Or is your company missing out on this? Put some strategy in place to strengthen this aspect of your company reputation to improve your talent lock.

# Release Tactic #4:
## *Discuss Transitions*

There are plenty of terrible ways to lose staff. They don't have to set their office on fire, have a meltdown in front of clients, or leave behind a mess of mismanaged paperwork in order to hurt us. Sometimes the most damaging way for someone to leave the team is **quietly**.

## The Danger of the Disappearing Employee

It happens in remote and traditional work teams alike: a team member suddenly disappears. The coworkers who shared daily responsibilities are often the least informed about reasons for and timeline of exit. In the worst cases, a colleague can disappear overnight with no warning and no explanation, emails bouncing with an unsettling "this person does not exist at your organization."

Every disappearing employee sends shockwaves through your culture. Even when there is ugly truth inside of a termination, hiding that truth doesn't make it any prettier. Whatever the implications of losing the team member are, clear and honest communication about the changes reduces the strain on the remaining team.

Silent departures can feed the insecurity of remaining staff members. Sinister speculation doesn't always land on the departing team member either; if no explanation is given, political overtones can be suspected, favoritism or bullying can be implied. Without clear communication, any number of inaccurate (and unhelpful) types of chatter emerge.

In the best situations, team member departures are shared in advance with the team, and the appropriate teammates work together to ensure continuity of knowledge as that person leaves. But whatever happens, positive and authentic communication about changing staff is necessary for top team performance.

## Team-Centric Transition Planning

If you break radio silence and shift toward a transparent termination process, it opens up a world of possibilities that strengthen onboarding and retention of new employees dramatically. This is because both the team member who is leaving and the team they're leaving behind can be involved in the replacement planning process. It also creates an opportunity for leaders to deal with the questions and stress in the culture surrounding the workload shifts and changes.

So let's talk about the most common kinds of team-centric transitions that all companies need to make at one point or another. We can divide them into quadrants depending on whether the employee who is leaving is sudden or planned, cooperative or hostile.

### Sudden, Hostile Departure

This is the employee who decides not to show up, and never shows up again. It also includes any employee who has violated the terms of their employment in such a way that they need to be terminated immediately and/or removed from the team without continued contact.

### Planned, Hostile Departure

This employee may say something like "here's my two weeks' notice and I'll be taking my ten days of PTO while I finish up my time here." And sometimes it includes someone who serves the full countdown of their departure, but doesn't care what shape they leave the team in when they go. This person may phone it in, handling the bare minimum, or they may actively cause mischief and mess as a parting gift.

## Sudden, Cooperative Departure

Often these individuals leave because of changes in their life circumstances. Caregiving demands, relocation, or even an advantageous opportunity can give our team members a reason to leave that they can't pass up. Their hands may be tied, but if they try to leave you in the best shape they can, you can accomplish some important things during their speedy departure.


## Planned, Cooperative Departure

This doesn't have to be someone who has been drinking the culture Kool-Aid. These aren't magical creatures that exist at other companies but never yours. If a team member gives intentional notice and isn't hostile to the team they're leaving behind, you'll gain more out of their offboarding process if you treat them as cooperative.

Whatever quadrant the offboarding employee falls in, do these things to release well:

1. **Avoid Scapegoating.**

It's especially tempting to do this with hostile exits. The stress and lost productivity of a hostile exit is not small. But is it actually that person's fault we're missing our deadline? Is their disorganization to blame for systemic problems with our team's processes, communication patterns, or overall productivity? Probably not. Dumping pent up frustration on the person who's leaving can seem like a safe way to acknowledge your stress because they're not around to hear or feel your emotion dump. But it's like emptying your trash can on the conference room table—that frustration has been amplified into the shared space in an unconstructive way.

2. **Take Ownership of Negative Factors.**

Whether it's pressure on performance, tough deadlines, strain added from the customers or stakeholders, or something else entirely, sometimes negative factors contributed to losing the employee. If we fail to acknowledge this, we risk amplifying the burnout remaining employees experience. They may think "so-and-so is the smart one; they got out of this place." By acknowledging the negative factors, you begin the process of addressing things that could result in more talent loss in the weeks and months to come.

## 3. **Praise The Praiseworthy.**

Expressing respect, gratitude, or praise for something the person who is offboarding contributed to the team contributes to the reservoir of positive regard on the team. Maybe you have to reach back to remember some of the highlights, that's okay. Bring them back to mind anyway. Even if someone has become hostile, or has been dragging their weight around for a while, acknowledging the good that they've brought to the team helps to pave a healthy way for someone new to enter and bring their best to the team.

## 4. **Address the Transition Period.**

If this employee's offboarding means any shift in responsibilities for other team members, directly address this. Don't assume that "if they're team players they won't complain." And don't presume that the workload will naturally redistribute itself. Invite team members to collaborate on the best way to navigate the transition period, whether it's a few days or a few months, this conversation can reduce the losses that grow while you're finding someone new. Even if you have a replacement employee ready to go, the training and onboarding of the new employee, and verification that all the workload from the previous employee is adequately handled, will call for a shift in duties for the rest of the team. If onboarding is handled exclusively by leadership or managers, this can be as minimal as checking in with team members for feedback in case they see any missed connections or gaps in the process from their seat on the team.

Shine the light on the exit and watch the confidence and vitality of your entire team improve. Remember as the leader, you are either creating a ripple of trust, respect, and calm or you're allowing distrust and anxiety to grow in the stillness.

# Take Action:

This tactic is all about authentic communication around employees who leave. Wherever you are in your organization, there is something you can do to improve the transition for yourself and others. Here are some action steps as examples. Use them as a springboard to imagine more ways to put energy back into the culture rather than allowing each departure to ramp up the stress.

### If You're on the Frontline:

- Notice when you are tempted to scapegoat or complain; this will only increase your stress. You will increase your physical and mental resilience if you make the effort to express gratitude for something positive that person brought to the team, and spend the stress points on addressing the workload or process problems instead.

- Find ways to contribute to the planning and feedback process the next time your team loses someone. If you have questions or concerns about the workload distribution or maybe a negative factor that is affecting you as well, don't just push them down until you burnout; look for opportunities to help improve things for yourself and others.

### If You're a Manager or Supervisor:

- Stop sweeping information about employee departures under the rug. Even if it is necessary for them to go, their exit will impact their colleagues psychologically, socially, and energetically. They are not children, or inmates; communicate with them like the professionals they are so they can contribute to the transition effectively.

- Verbalize appreciation for the employee who is leaving in some form. Acknowledge their contribution, and wherever possible give specific reminders of something positive and / or meaningful they shared with the company while they were there.

### If You're an Executive Leader:

- Review the employees who have left your organization and evaluate what kinds of exits are most common. Do you have a lot of sudden, hostile departures? This is a driver of continued talent loss since it puts extra strain on the team. Are none of them planned? This can be a sign that your management staff need training or strategy for ongoing mentoring and coaching where they see and deal with problems as they develop.

- Look at the example you set in your leadership with how ex-employees are talked about. Do they get scapegoated for as long as possible for all the things that went wrong while they were there? Or are they metaphorically tossed out of the moving company car and never thought of again? Make the effort to verbalize the value and meaning of the next employee to leave the company. This culture shift is a game changer.

# Release Tactic #5:
## *Release with Gratitude*

One of the last things we feel when an employee is leaving is gratitude. Whether they were an awesome teammate or a dead weight, letting them go means work and disruption while we fill their place or redistribute their duties to other employees.

But if you want to create a talent lock at your organization, showing gratitude—especially to employees who are leaving the company—is a powerful way to start. In valuing these employees and verbalizing the meaningful value they brought to the team while they were there, we boost the gratitude in our organization's culture.

When we show appreciation to workers who are employed at our companies, staff can feel like our praise is somewhat self-serving. "Are they grateful for me, or for the cash I put in their wallet today?" But when an employee is leaving, and you thank them for all they've brought to the company, you walk the talk of valuing gratitude in your culture to a person who doesn't expect it.

But why should we bother? If someone is leaving our company, what's the point of ending on a positive note with them?

Most leaders who have been in business long enough, know how long a bad employee exit can haunt your company. Whether it's ongoing bad blood, or a slowly growing negative trend in the company's reputation in the community, ex-employees continue to influence our standing. Sometimes their experiences influence who is willing to work for us in the future, whether we can get the best talent, and even how positively (or negatively) our customers come to feel about us as a company.

But beyond that, there is something dehumanizing about the revolving door of turnover in our organizations. If we fail to express gratitude to the employees who are leaving, it communicates to the remaining staff that they're just replaceable widgets in a machine. This drives disengagement for those left behind.

## Gratitude is a Superfood

Gratitude has long been studied in psychology and behavioral neuroscience. It's seen as a superfood emotion, because when we practice gratitude it has a measurable impact on our brain's performance, our physical health, and our social connectedness.[12] They say gratitude is the antidote to all of our problems. There's something to that.

Though practicing gratitude bears dividends at every season of an employee's life, when they're offboarding it can be easy to forget it. In the face of the stress of replacing someone, we can forget to channel gratitude toward them for what they've done.

Don't miss this opportunity to show gratitude. Often, leaders who practice gratitude while offboarding team members experience less stress during the transition process, and have more optimism and ease in moving through the change.

Part of your success formula for creating a talent lock culture is staying in touch with the meaning and value that the humans in your organization are creating. Force yourself to notice the gratitude-worthy efforts of the employee during their tenure, and it will balance your perspective as you move forward to strengthen your team.

Even if you're not in a position to enact any of the other Release tactics when someone leaves your organization, you can put in the effort to notice and express your gratitude for them. If your organization "disappears" employees, you can still practice gratitude on your own, and speak well of what you appreciated about that person to someone else. Simply doing that will help you begin to experience the benefits of gratitude to lift the load in the wake of losing a colleague.

In 2021 and 2022, I was honored to participate with Quint Studer in his Gratitude Symposium. He gathered over 50 leaders to speak and share on the topic of gratitude and we served tens of thousands of people across the globe. What I witnessed in that process was how gratitude's benefits were so extensive and nuanced that we spent a month exploring the topic with leaders. Even small efforts to increase the gratitude quotient at your organization can have shocking ripple effects for you and your team.

## Gather Gratitude Regularly

Savvy professionals know our memory will fail us, especially when it comes to details from the busy interactions at work each day. That's why it's essential to establish some system for recording notes on the people you interact with regularly.

Digital solutions for keeping data on your contacts come in a million different flavors. Something as simple as the address book on your phone can offer a "notes" section that you can fill with information as time goes by. But for most of us we need something a bit more robust. We need a place to put the info, as well as reminders to add to it.

If you're leading or mentoring someone, set up recurring reminders or tasks to make a quick note every thirty, sixty, or ninety days. I know one entrepreneur who schedules recurring emails to herself to record gratitude about each of her contractors at regular intervals. Another puts gratitude appointments in his Outlook calendar. Try something and see what happens.

Writing down something you appreciate about how someone showed up to their first day, what you saw them handling very well at their competency review after their first ninety days, and from your regular coaching sessions gives you a powerful list of memories to draw from when they get ready to move on.

The key is intentional effort to be consistent and not random. Use the gift of your electronic calendar to trigger prompts to your future self, and reminders of the ideas at the moment you can use them. Your team will think you have a great memory and wonder how you did it.

# The Gratitude Tax

I've noticed something unexpected pops up for managers who embrace mentoring and use gratitude practice to show value to their employees—there's a gratitude tax that takes a chunk out of the negative energy in the workplace! It strengthens our own sense of an employee's strengths, and helps us lean into leading them rather than dismissing them as "poor performers."

Over the years, I've heard John Maxwell as he teaches his 101 Principle. The principle teaches that we would be wise to find the one thing we like and give it 100% of our attention. What would happen if you found something admirable or effective, something valuable about each of your employees and put gratitude energy into watching it grow?

My grandmother taught me to never say anything bad about others, even if they deserve it. I watched her live this way in spite of the excuses I knew she had to complain. Unlike those of us who can only hold back negative comments so long before they explode on others, her bedrock of gratitude gave her consistency and patience to serve others without breaking her values.

We don't want to admit it, but our memories are flawed. If we don't make an effort to notice and record the positive behaviors, attitudes, and efforts of our employees we can wimp out of leading them, developing them, and challenging them to become all they can.

Most leaders who begin practicing gratitude and combine it with regular praise see a significant slow down on turnover. Grateful praise is such a powerful talent lock strategy that I'll be as direct as to say this: if you don't have a regular gratitude practice I guarantee that some of the turnover you have now is unnecessary.

But if it's gotten to the end and you're losing someone, it's still the right time to start expressing that gratitude. If nothing else, it will help you improve your own energy loss from the offboarding process. Losing employees is draining. Engage the superfood emotion of gratitude and you'll see your energy restore more swiftly.

Let's bring *sapere vedere* into the conversation of gratitude. Using your hindsight capability, reflect on when someone else showed gratitude toward you? What did they say or share? How did you feel or respond? Were they consistent in their sharing or was it a random act?

How did this ripple through the team they led? Now looking forward, who do you want to keep on your team? What can you or should you do differently in your gratitude attitude toward them? Now use this insight to elevate your gratitude game. Start today!

## Take Action:

This tactic is all about using gratitude to reduce energy losses during offboarding. Wherever you are in your organization, there is something you can do to engage gratitude around your colleagues, even if they are leaving. Here are some action steps as examples. Use them as a springboard to imagine more ways to let gratitude ease transitions.

**If You're on the Frontline:**

- If there is stress on the team because someone is underperforming or leaving the team, practice gratitude to protect your own energy and avoid scapegoating them (or others).

- If you are in a toxic workplace and planning a change, practice honest gratitude in some form by identifying something each person you worked with did that you are grateful for. This is especially necessary for the unfair boss, the bully coworker, and anyone else who seemed to make life hard. If you can leave with gratitude it reduces the drain on your energy as you move forward.

**If You're a Manager or Supervisor:**

- Map a simple strategy for recording and remembering things to be grateful for. This could be notes in a calendar, recurring emails you send to yourself and add to over time, or a set of notes you reference before coaching sessions or meetings with your staff. Start recording specific things you can be grateful about for each person on your team.

- Bring to mind the employees who most recently left your team (for any reason.) Identify things you are grateful for toward that employee from the time they were there and make an effort to express that gratitude to someone else on your team. Whether their name comes up at work still, or is avoided like it's taboo, speak of them with gratitude.

**If You're an Executive Leader:**

- Model a grateful release the next time an employee is laid off or fired by directly addressing the team left behind about the change in staff and expressing the value that employee brought. If you didn't manage this person directly, **ask coworkers and managers to** help you identify their admirable traits and or specifics of their contribution.

- Make a call or write a personal note to staff you directly manage when they leave the company and include specific gratitude for their contribution. Establish a process for this to happen for every person who leaves, with gratitude flowing from their direct supervisor and/or peers.

# Attraction: Be a Talent Magnet



Hiring can start to feel like a mad scramble to wrangle an unbearable office workload. But however desperate you are to increase your staffing levels, remember: your mindset about the people on your team will bleed through to new employee prospects. These five talent attraction tactics will strengthen the culture of the team you already have in ways specifically designed to draw top-shelf talent to your team.

Seeing the value and potential in every person who joins your team has to be more than a platitude. Do better than filling a job description; be ready to offer your buy-in as a leader, colleague, or employee. If you're the CEO, your attitude about people ripples all the way to the frontline. Your number one responsibility as a leader is to draw out the best in those you do or will lead.

But even if you're not in a position of leadership, you can impact how attractive your organization is to new talent. Fight past the burnout and exhaustion you may be feeling to get excited about the potential of the new human joining the team.

Some of us have already lost too many staff members, or have outgrown our teams. If you're in the market to hire high performers, your organization needs effective attraction skills. Even with a strong compensation offer, today's highly mobile workforce won't say yes to your company if your organization is making the same mistakes as their previous employer.

Every company has limits on what they can offer in pay and benefits. But management by paycheck is failing in every sector. These five attraction tactics will optimize your chance of getting the truly great team players hidden in the noise of the applicant pool. It starts with your employment brand, broadcasts in the job ad, and draws high quality people through promises of personal and professional development.

## Which Tactics Can I Skip?

I'm the first one to cut the fluff. Clients who work with me can sense I never suggest anything just for the kumbaya effect. I still have the eye to efficiency and essentialism gained from more than a decade of active-duty Army service. My proving ground for team building came through recruiting for a company building a healthcare service line for hospital leaders. Between the military and healthcare, I've become brutally honest about what is necessary to meet your company's success objectives.

I've personally conducted tens of thousands of interviews over the years. I have helped hundreds of companies improve their hiring practices. That's where I'm coming from as I suggest the following five attraction tactics:

1.  Build Your Employment Brand
2.  Develop a WHO sCOREcard
3.  Sharpen Your Job Ads
4.  Interview as a Team
5.  Close the Deal or Close the Loop

There isn't a single part of that list that is fluff or just for companies trying to be known as touchy-feely places to work.

## Start With Reflection

Before putting the employee search machinery to work on finding talent, block an hour to reflect on why this role is open. If you're filling in the vacancies created by turnover, get curious about why the previous employee(s) left. Avoid scapegoating them and look for insights into workflow process, training effectiveness, and mentoring and support for that role.

Employees get burnt out in a role where they believe the work they're asked to do everyday is different from the work they thought they were hired for. Investigate each instance of turnover for signs of this. Companies who do this often don't realize they are putting false advertising into their job ads. They often have a disconnect between the team members responsible for hiring and the managers who oversee and set the workload for the employee once they start.

Maybe you aren't filling the role due to turnover or maybe your organization has simply grown. Congratulations! Reflection in this circumstance gives you the chance to think about what true value this role being filled will create. Resist hiring based solely on skills with a drive to get workload handled; set some culture and teamwork goals for this new role.

If you're re-starting the hiring process because a job vacancy is tough to fill, do a different kind of reflection. Get curious about what your employee candidates think of your employment brand. Do the talented individuals you want to hire have a bad opinion of what it's like to work at your company? Do they have no idea you even exist? How can you get on their radar in new or innovative ways?

Your number one goal if replacing is to up-level the talent, or if expanding to hire someone who will be your next star. Hire for values fit not skill set, to elevate your team.

# Attraction Tactic #1:
## *Build Your Employment Brand*

When you think about your company's brand, chances are, you think of name recognition, marketing power, and the experience **for customers**. Consumer branding is important; but nothing drives your company's success the way that your employment branding does. Whether you know it or not, your company has a brand as an employer. When it comes time to bring in new talent, it's the clarity, quality, and strength of your employment brand that influences your candidate pool.

A strong reputation opens doors to new customers. It does the same for increasing your access to new employees. Word of mouth about your company as an employer can motivate strong employees to gravitate toward your company.

Think about the average person in need of a new or better job. Most individuals who have quick success connecting to a strong, highly attractive opportunity do so through their warm network. A friend, or often a friend-of-a-friend connects the dots to give access to a great opportunity.

But the individual isn't the only party who needs something good from the job market. Your company needs to find strong candidates and solid hires in order for your company's bottom line and continued growth. Just like the individual applicants go through their network and build off of reputation, your company has a reputation that can help or hinder you in making a good hire.

Who is out there saying your organization is a great place to work? What is it people would be drawn to your company for?

If you're like most struggling organizations, the only thing drawing people to you right now is a job's compensation package. People come to you for the pay. If money is the only reason for people to take a job at your company, you will have ongoing challenges when it comes time to lead them. If you want to hold them accountable, or urge them to fulfill their potential you will find few levers to push.

That's why success tactic number one for attracting top-notch talent to your organization is building an employment brand that motivates candidates to want to join you in the work you do.

Talented workers today are looking for organizations that help them reach their potential, and value what they have to offer. They're looking for a work home where they can make a difference and get their needs met.

Let's talk about the pieces that go into building this kind of work home.

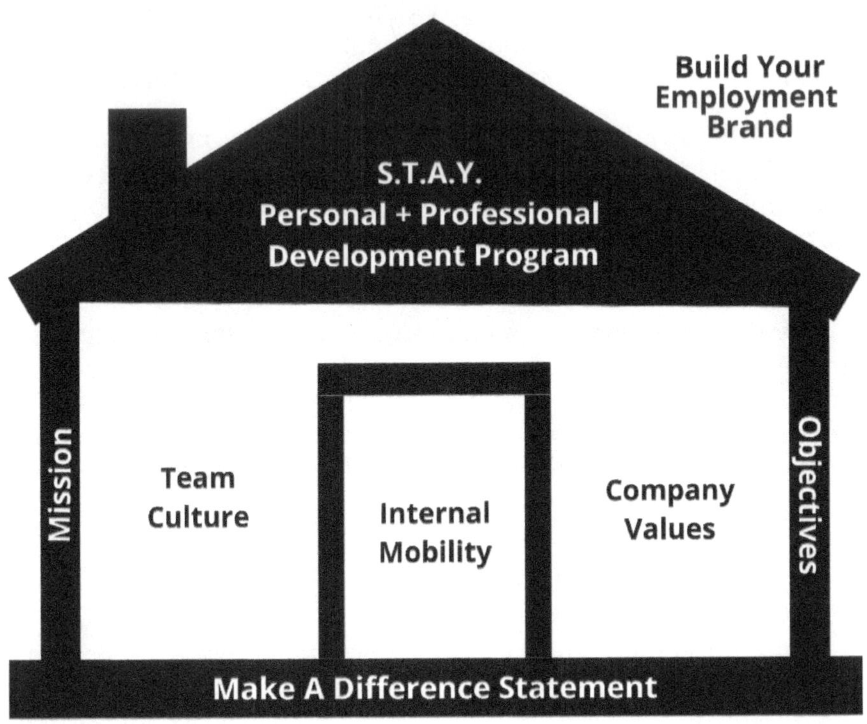

# Foundation: Make a Difference Statement

The foundation of your employment brand is something we can call your Make A Difference, or M.A.D. Statement. What's the difference your company makes for customers, employees, the community, the industry, and the world? Whether you're a social justice brand, a multi-site healthcare organization, tech startup, or a local bank, take the time to sharpen your M.A.D. Statement by thinking about these two questions:

**Who are you helping?**

**What problem do you solve?**

Your first few attempts at expressing this may sound vague. That's normal. But a general "we help people get healthier" is only a starting spot. If people are going to be intrinsically motivated to join you in the work you do, they need to see something compelling in your M.A.D. Statement.

For some organizations, the difference they're making isn't altruistic. Being the best at something, an industry leader or innovator may be less warm and fuzzy. That's fine. What matters is showing your employees an identity they can embrace and be passionate about at work.

A game development company may "rescue people from boredom" or a digital insights company may "help companies predict the future so they aren't wasting time on past trends." Even healthcare organizations can stand out by clarifying the difference they're making in a meaningful way such as "caring for individuals *as* individuals."

Start by bringing into focus the difference your company seeks to make in the marketplace and the world, and you'll trigger intrinsically motivated candidates to see the value in working with you. Intrinsic motivation is the key for employees who can be engaged and self-motivated if hired. They engage if the difference you're making is compelling to them.

# Structure: The Mission and Objectives

When it comes time to draft a compelling job ad (more on this in Tactic #3), you will structure your job ad using the mission and objectives of the specific role you want to fill. When it comes to individual roles, it can be easier to see the focused mission and objectives that that person on the team needs to fulfill.

But for your employment brand to be compelling, you need to step back and see the overarching mission of the company. If you're a huge organization, each major department can develop a clear reputation, a focused employment brand. For example, the trauma unit, hospice teams, and rehab services in a large hospital system may each develop individual culture and identity, to increase their magnetic pull on prospective employees. By projecting a clear brand for their department, more of **the right applicants** apply for new job openings. The departmental mission, culture, and objectives pre-qualified applicants who sensed they would thrive there.

For many teams, the employment brand paints a picture of the work being done by your team and the meaning created by your successes. A technology sales chain that only focuses on the tasks being done might paint an employment brand with the objective "we sell technology tools." If your teams are successful, they will indeed sell those technology tools. But that task-oriented approach is not compelling. Bring into focus the meaning created by that success and you might have a mission to "delight people and elevate their performance through technology."

Not only does a framework of meaningful objectives such as "delighting people" and "elevating people's performance" paint a different picture of what it's like to work at your organization, it also offers a pathway for training, accountability, and measuring success that can be repeated and amplified by your employees to increase effectiveness over time.

## Roof: S.T.A.Y. Development Program

Let's continue painting the picture of the work home you're creating for employees to come live in at your organization. The foundation is your Make a Difference Statement, and the Mission and Objectives for your company or department create the structure. The roof that protects the whole thing from the drought of burnout, and the ill weather of market forces is the structure you create for employee development.

If you read this book from the beginning, you'll have learned about the S.T.A.Y. Development Program in the Retention section. If you haven't seen it yet, feel free to flip back and review. When it comes to building an employment brand, recognize that the professional development opportunities your company extends to new employee candidates offer them protection and safety going into the future.

A paycheck is only worth so much if an employee comes to work at an organization where their skills aren't developed, their knowledge doesn't grow, and they aren't given room to take opportunities and expand their value. Even if you hire an employee who is on top of their game this week, what they know will be outdated at some point. If they're going to stay shiny and sharp they need to continue to grow.

But what if your company doesn't provide growth opportunities, doesn't include any time in your weekly schedule to learn, or doesn't provide connections to mentors and resources that deepen your knowledge? It means you will have to go outside of your job to grow.

Some employees do this by growing during their time off. If this is necessary it will only be a matter of time before your employee has to leave your company in order to keep growing. If instead, every year spent at your company is one where they become more skilled, confident, and valuable as an employee, healthier and more energized as a person, they have a lot of reasons to stay with you.

This creates an employee value proposition that is bigger than the paycheck, and will bring you better quality candidates regardless of the competition you have. Employees today are looking for jobs that will add value back to them, both as an individual and a professional. If you want to attract a higher quality of employee, don't skip this part.

As various research continues to validate, employees favor companies that develop them. With the fast pace of our economy, and changes in the marketplace, technology, and social life, employees are constantly scrambling to keep up. Gone are the days when your college degree and typing speed were all that an employer looked at; now we have an alphabet soup of computer languages, and a growing cloud of technology we need our teams to interact with effectively.

No matter how strong and prepared a hiring prospect is when they arrive at your organization, the slow march of time is tarnishing their readiness for work in today's world. If your employees aren't gaining new skills every year, they are falling behind, and they know it.

Mastery doesn't occur in a weekend course, or an annual seminar. If your people are going to retain and expand their talent, ongoing systems for training and coaching make all the difference. Making this part of your employment brand sends the signal that your company will develop and grow their employees.

## The Door: Mobility & Advancement

Who wants to live in a house without doors? That would be a prison. The world of work has changed drastically over the past decade, with employee turnover at an accelerated pace. Much of that turnover is due to the fact that most companies do not provide internal mobility and job growth for existing employees. Employees with a growth drive have to do it elsewhere.

For many of our organizations, budgets and management teams are siloed even when company objectives require all parts of the company to integrate. Internal mobility can happen within a department, or across the aisle in another department. By keeping employees within your organization, elements of your team culture and organizational wisdom can be retained and extended. Long term, internal mobility can be the key to breaking down silos and improving the flow of communication as relationships are cross-pollinated by the employees who move from one role to another.

But why aren't we moving people around our organizations? It's often because we're treating employees like an expense that must be paid in order to execute a set amount of work, rather than seeing them as assets that can be developed and strengthened to be more valuable, productive, and efficient over time. We don't expect them to change for the better. We just use them up until they leave.

There's no point putting a door on a house that has no roof. If internal mobility is pointless or impossible at your organization, it's likely because your company is failing to develop and equip the employees you have now. The more you unlock each employee's potential and help them achieve mastery through intentional growth, the more possibilities will arise for using their strengths in your organization. Without effective mentoring and leadership practices, you will not be aware of the potential value in employees.

If you want to be an employer of choice, people need to see that working hard for your company results in increased opportunity, and the potential to advance. The best employees are ones who use what experts call "discretionary effort" to achieve and solve problems in their daily work. What makes an employee choose to do more than is required or expected? They need to see some meaning or value in continued success. Being recognized for their efforts and offered opportunities to grow and advance are the kinds of motivators that can unlock this on your team.

## Oxygen: Company Culture & Team Values

In every organization, culture is the air we breathe. The attitudes, energy, and values that are honored in your workplace set the atmosphere for life at work. Certain mindsets and behaviors characterize the team you have assembled so far, and they determine who will thrive in and contribute positively to the company if hired.

The hard part about culture is that you have one. It's there, whether you've tried to make one or not. Culture doesn't wait for you to pick it, and is slow to respond to ideology (saying things like "we're like a family here") that isn't lived out in practice (if the work environment is completely cut-throat and transactional).

What's in the air at your organization?

In some ways this is the hardest part of the employment brand to create because you cannot bring it to life in a workshop or leadership strategy session. It has to be developed between and among the team members you currently have, and transferred to new employees when they arrive.

If you have major air quality issues in your organization, decisive hiring can help you change the air. Take for example a healthcare organization whose employees have become distrustful of management, who fail to speak up to help improve things or take ownership in solving problems, and who have high levels of burnout. To turn the culture around, hire new employees who can expect to help management improve the way things work by speaking up and helping to solve problems. But if you do this, your leadership team will need to actively work to respond to feedback and create new experiences in the culture. The tide can turn faster with the help of new employees if it's supported by the leadership in a consistent way.

Decide what kind of culture you want on your team and go to work shifting the tide of culture you have toward your intention. Few things make a larger difference in your company's reputation to potential employees than a vibrant culture at work.

## Put it All Together: Your Employment Brand

I like using the house to illustrate the pieces of the employment brand. It helps with thinking it through and identifying where your current brand is vulnerable. Think about your employment house for a second. Do you have a solid foundation—a Make A Difference Statement that every employee could verbalize easily? Do people know what the Mission and Objectives of your organization are so they can feel confident and driven every day when they show up for work?

Maybe your employment house is missing the roof, and the sunburn of burnout is hitting your people because they aren't growing, achieving mastery, and unlocking their potential as you develop them. Or maybe your company has become a prison, each employee locked in the cell of the job they were hired for with no hope of advancement or mobility unless they "escape" by quitting.

Take a moment to capture the pieces of your employment brand.

**What difference do you make (and for whom)?**

**What is your company mission?**

**What are your company's short- and long-term objectives?**

**How are employees developed as people and professionals here?**

_______________________________________________

_______________________________________________

**What opportunities do you offer for internal mobility and advancement?**

_______________________________________________

_______________________________________________

**What attitudes, mindsets, behaviors, and values are in the company culture?**

_______________________________________________

_______________________________________________

## Take Action:

This tactic is all about becoming an employer of choice. Wherever you are in your organization, there is something you can do to participate in and spread a positive culture to attract quality new employees. Here are some action steps as examples. Use them as a springboard to imagine more ways to help your organization become a place where employees thrive and stay.

**If You're on the Frontline:**
- Find something positive you can say about the company you work at, pass it on to a friend or work connection. Become part of the word-of-mouth that helps draw great new people to the company in the future.

- One of the biggest things you can do to reduce your own burnout and keep increasing in your value where you work is to take advantage of opportunities to learn, grow, and participate in different initiatives where you're at. Check the company website, actually read the next corporate email blast, and ask your leaders what growth opportunities exist. If nothing does, have a discussion with your leader or manager about creating some growth opportunities for you and your team.

**If You're a Manager or Supervisor:**

- Check in on the mission of your organization and see how easily each of your employees can express it. How can you help your team understand the mission as something everyone pursues each day at work?

- If one area of your "employment house" had the biggest weakness, which would it be? Are there no doors of internal mobility? No roof of systematic employee development? Bad air of culture issues? What is something you can do from your place in the organization to improve things?

**If You're an Executive Leader:**

- Assess the employment brand you already have as a company. Get input from outside the company, and ask questions of current employees in a way that makes them feel safe to give honest feedback about the positives and negatives of company culture. Use these insights to see where your attraction power can improve.

- Use the reflection on the previous pages to put together a clear picture of the kind of house your company wants to offer employees. Elevate your vision about what is possible in the next decade and strategize how to move your organization in that direction.

# Attraction Tactic #2:
## *Develop a WHO sCOREcard*

What if I could give you a magic blueprint for finding the right person for your team? Not just a dream list of positive attributes to toss into a job ad—an actual answer key to guide confident choices about which candidates to spend time interviewing, and who will perform long term? This kind of blueprint would eliminate months of limbo, and sometimes years of trial and error as you try to find staff that can rock the role you've put them in.

That blueprint is what my team and I call a WHO sCOREcard. The WHO—the right human to hire—is brought into clear focus by clarifying the CORE purpose, values, and behaviors of the role you're filling. Pulled together in the tool, they provide a scorecard you can hold up to potential candidates to select the right people to interview and hire. Using the blueprint, you'll pull better candidates from the stack of résumés.

Every leader and team who employs this tactic and creates a WHO sCOREcard for themselves sees transformation in their hiring process. The kind of reflective writing that goes into creating your blueprint for each role you want to fill isn't easy, but it is the right kind of hard. I'll walk you through the process in this section.

Escape the constant churn of weak hires and unnecessary turnover by investing forethought and planning to create this WHO sCOREcard. This is one way of practicing *sapere vedere*. Use hindsight to evaluate the results you've been getting, pull insights about WHO you need, and what the CORE of success in this role will be, and you will have foresight mapped out in the finished blueprint for who will do well with you. Once you've created this for one position, it becomes a template that can be customized to serve each position in your organization.

You'll also gain clarity as you create the sCOREcard for the position, which lays groundwork for the onboarding process. This focused picture of what the core of the role is (the values, behaviors, and purpose of the role), guides the new hire as they begin. It paints a powerful picture of what is expected of them, and goes beyond vague platitudes to help them know how to live out their role with excellence. This foundation establishes a pathway for accountability before the applicant even walks in the door.

## Find the WHO and the CORE for your next hire:

When most leaders start "the hiring process," their process for selection is random at best, rushed and scattered at worst. They have no consistency in questions for multiple candidates and no subjective way to select the best fit.

The WHO sCOREcard is everything you want to know about the person who will be a good fit, and what skills are pivotal to their success. We intentionally start with mission and values before moving to behaviors and outcomes because it is crucial to get to the core of the hire right.

What is the core of the person? The inside thinking and behaviors, not the outside visible skills or education, will influence your work environment. None of the externals matter if the person's core would sour your culture. Clients confide in me, their coach, that "the employee is really skilled...but they're a miserable human." Skill is clearly not enough since this person increases the misery quotient in the culture. Hire people who are good at what they do, but great at who they are.

To fill out your own hiring blueprint, you will clarify the following about the role you intend to fill:

- The Behaviors the Candidate Needs Skill In
- Core Competencies That Must be Demonstrated
- Outcomes and Objectives to be Achieved in the Role

You can use this information to develop WHO Identifier Questions that can be used to screen and interview applicants. These questions are designed to shine the light on the values, behaviors, and competencies the candidates possess.

1.  **What is the core purpose of this role?**

    This is the step of envisioning the mission of this role. Think big picture, and paint a clear description of the meaning created by the person in this position. How does this role drive value, mitigate risk, or stabilize growth in your organization? Beyond the tasks to be done, what is the value of this role being carried out with excellence?

2.  **What are the core values of your team?**

    This step connects you to the values you want to cultivate in your company culture. How does a member of this team need to think, learn, collaborate, interact, and communicate? What is essential to the character and motivation of the person you hire so that they thrive and contribute to the thriving of their teammates?

3.  **What are the core behaviors of this role?**

    Take the values you have identified and ask what kind of behaviors would flow from an employee living out that value. What would be the consistent actions, habits, and processes you want to see this role maintain? What key need does it fill, resource does it create, or workflow does it keep running smoothly? What kinds of processes, projects and priorities will be managed from this seat on your team?

## Make This Blueprint Come Alive

At some point, we have to pull those company values off the wall and breathe life into them. One way to do that is to give yourself and your teams freedom to embody those big values in team-specific or role-specific ways.

Ask yourself, "what does our corporate value of transparency mean for the customer service team?" or "how can our technical team display a hospitable spirit even though they don't interact with customers directly?" Questions like that often broaden employees' understanding of what a value means, and they discover living it impacts their quality of life as a worker, not just the customer experience as an end user.

When you build this hiring blueprint, take each core value and describe the set of behaviors that embody the way the value is meant to be lived out for that role.

When you are choosing values, be descriptive, using powerful, meaningful titles. Instead of listing things like "ownership, accountability, communication," consider "absolute ownership, proactive accountability, positive communication." Define each inspiring title to paint a clear picture of what it means to live that value or fulfill that competency.

# Sample Mission:

### The Mission for a Nurse Manager of Clinical Services

Compassionate clinical nurse manager dedicated to ensuring continuity of care for all patients according to our clinic's values. Main responsibilities include ensuring capable staff is in place to provide excellent care and service to patients and their families, and facilitating the assessment and equipping of staff to maintain our ability to deliver the best care in our community. This nurse manager will be trained and equipped with the knowledge, tools, and expectations to excel as a team member at our clinic and to transfer their knowledge effectively to colleagues.

### The Mission for a Customer Service Manager

Warm and engaging customer service manager to lead by example in our fast-paced sales support department at a socially conscious clothing label. Core skills include de-escalating conflict, mentoring, and skills-transferal capacity, maintaining accurate records and data security, and experience-based knowledge in dealing with retail customer complaints.

## The Mission for an Information Securities Analyst

Mentally agile information security analyst with experience in online retail systems to support growth and expansion while safeguarding critical data against attacks and system failures. Main responsibilities include securing critical data with prevention-oriented solutions to help our company maintain the zero-breach status we have worked so hard to achieve.

# Sample CORE Values & Competencies

## Sample Value: Driving Continuous Improvement

Demonstrates the ability to implement ways to measurably improve the quality of systems, processes, and procedures in an effort to improve the organization's overall performance.

## Sample Value: Proactive Accountability

Takes responsibility for one's actions. Does not blame others but rather works proactively to correct errors regardless of the cause. Takes ownership for projects and tasks assigned. Develops solutions to current and anticipated problems within industry regulations and guidelines provided by leadership.

## Sample Value: Self-Motivation

Demonstrates experience in directing oneself to accomplish goals and objectives, overcoming obstacles and demonstrating perseverance to see a project through to completion. Shows self-efficacy and ownership of goals, rather than needing to be pushed by a supervisor.

## Sample Value: Detail Orientation

Demonstrates the ability to complete all tasks with great attention to accuracy, regardless of magnitude. Shows process(es) for effectively managing and accomplishing all details necessary to complete a project or assignment. Takes proper ownership of communicating information or concerns regarding detail management on shared projects to serve the organization's best interests.

## Sample Competency: Lean Manufacturing

Demonstrates expertise in effective techniques designed to improve manufacturing processes in terms of efficiency, cost reduction, enhanced quality, and related metrics. Shows skill and expertise in such models as 5S, Toyota Production System, Six Sigma, and value stream mapping.

## Sample Competency: Employee Relationship Development / Coaching

Demonstrates ability to accurately assess and identify an individual's growth opportunities. Provides timely guidance, feedback, and encouragement to help employees strengthen specific knowledge and skills needed to achieve optimal performance and achieve short- and long-term organizational goals.

## Sample Competency: Systems Thinking

Demonstrates the ability to integrate various business operations and processes. Does not act with silo or functional thinking. Is able to see all the pieces of the operational puzzle and determine how they fit together. Expresses a spirit of partnering with other functional areas to ensure overall organizational success and goal attainment.

These examples are designed to show how competencies need to be clarified with specific, meaning-oriented descriptions that show how the value is created.

# Develop Interview Questions

Once you've envisioned the value, and defined what you and your team mean by each one, you're ready to craft questions to search for applicants who demonstrate them during screening and interviews. Chances are there are a lot of areas you need to assess candidates in, and quickly.

If you don't use some structure to distribute your questions across every category, you are likely to fill the interview with questions that



## Interview Holistically

**S.** Standards

**E.** Experience / Education

**A.** Attitude of Willingness

**R.** Results Achieved

**C.** Cognitive / Competencies

**H.** Habits of Consistency

Ask questions in each area to fully assess candidates for strengths and fit.

Gaps discovered during an interview can become training goals, or disqualify interviewees.

focus on only a couple of areas. The result can be a false positive on a candidate who has major deficiencies in the areas you failed to probe. This is how many good leaders make bad hires. To help you distribute your questions effectively so that you can assess candidates thoroughly, use the acrostic S.E.A.R.C.H.

**S.E.A.R.C.H.** stands for **S**tandards, **E**xperience/**E**ducation, **A**ttitude of Willingness, **R**esults Achieved, **C**ognitive/**C**ompetency Skills, **H**abits of Consistency. If you create up to three questions in each category, you will get a living snapshot of what that candidate will be capable of if hired by your organization.

Below are examples of the kinds of questions that help uncover these essential behaviors in hiring prospects. I have left many of them industry-specific since specificity is key. Pivot the focus to your industry and role with the same kind of specificity.

## Standards:

What standards do your values make important in this role? Choose questions to help you identify what standards the candidate has experience upholding, or is intrinsically motivated to pursue. Some roles require high integrity toward standards of communication, confidentiality, quality, or responsiveness. One of the main areas management by paycheck is failing in most in modern workplaces is in the area of standards. A paycheck may get someone to punch a clock and check a box, but an employee who strives to meet the standard needs to be bought in.

Sample Value: **Proactive Accountability**

Sample Questions:

- "Tell me about a time when the directions you were given to perform a task were not clear. What did you do?"
- "What are the regulations that impact your work, and how do you stay up-to-date on those?"
- "When was the last time your boss gave you some negative or constructive feedback about your job performance? What was the feedback and how did you respond?"
- "When was the last time you had to admit a mistake or own up to a lack of follow through?"


## Experience & Education:

What experience and/or education is necessary to do this job well? Choose questions to confirm and explore the kinds of training, mentoring, and hands-on experience your candidate has in key competencies. Identify the level of knowledge and skill required to even consider a candidate, and make note of areas where you are willing to develop and train them on the job.

Sample Competency: **Lean Manufacturing**

Sample Questions:

- "Tell me about some specific improvements you were able to deliver using lean initiative."
- "How do you stay current on the most advanced lean manufacturing techniques?"

- "How have you gained cost reductions from process improvements in the past?"
- "Looking back on a major lean initiative you were involved with, what did you learn that would have changed your approach next time?"

## Attitude of Willingness:

What attitude and willingness does the applicant need to demonstrate? Attitude is one of the main factors in how this candidate will impact your culture if hired. Willingness and positive attitudes are also key markers for an intrinsically motivated, growth-oriented individual. I haven't come across a job yet where teachability and willingness to work hard weren't a huge portion of feeding success for the team.

Sample Value: **Self-Motivation**

Sample Questions:

- "Tell me about a time you recognized and acted on a problem before others."
- "How do you assess your own performance? In other words, how do you know if you are doing a good job?"
- "Tell me about a situation where you had to overcome someone else's objection to your work. How did you handle it?"
- "How do you plan your project assignments? Can you give me a recent example?"

## Results Achieved:

What previous results demonstrate mastery and competence? Choose questions to help you identify accomplishments this candidate has had part in achieving that show they will be able to achieve in this new role. Keep an eye out for candidates who manage to communicate confidently and passionately about the difference they helped make, while acknowledging others who contributed to the success. Employees who feel positive ownership of the results they've achieved in the past, and who can share credit with team members are likely to be intrinsically motivated and a positive addition to the team at your organization.

Sample Competency: **Employee Relationship Development / Coaching**

Sample Questions:

- "What experience do you have preparing others to take over a role, or improve their competency in the workplace?"
- "Tell me about a time a colleague has sought your advice on a challenge they were having at work? What was the situation and how did you advise them?"
- "Tell me about a time when you experienced friction with a team member. What kind of feedback or communication did you use with them to help improve their performance or teamwork?"
- "How have you found that people most effectively learn new skills or behaviors?"

## Cognitive/Competency Skills:

How does this person need to think, and what do they need to be able to do to thrive here? This starts with understanding what kind of mental habits bring success in the role and team you want to hire this person for. You can't assess it in an interview if you don't know what you're looking for! But taking time to prepare questions to investigate the cognitive and competency skills of candidates drastically improves how accurate your prediction of a candidate's success is. The way they think, and what they are able to do, will determine their value on your team.

Sample Competency: **Systems Thinking**

Sample Questions:

- "Have you had to deal with peers who might operate with a silo mentality? Take me through a specific situation and what you did to address it."
- "Tell me about your experience dealing with inventory planning, logistics, and sales within your company? Have you been able to influence any of these areas, assuming they did not report to you?"
- "Tell me about a time when you made a decision that took other functional areas of the organization into account."
- "How do you avoid the tendency to think in your own functional area without considering the workflow and impact on other departments?"

## Habits of Consistency:

What habits will be essential for this person's success and consistent performance? Most mindful leaders know it's our habits that determine our success, not the occasional efforts we make. That's why I'm shocked how many leaders do nothing to assess a candidate's current habits. Habits are hard to form and tough to break, so chances are the habits your candidate has now will continue when they start with you. Go beyond deliverables and achievements to check for habits of consistency, since they are the framework for growth and the mechanism of momentum.

Sample Value: **Detail Orientation**

Sample Questions:

- "What are some of the tasks you have been assigned that have not really held your interest, or which seemed boring. How did you ensure those tasks were done well and on time?"
- "Tell me about a typical day for you." (Look for elements of planning, structure, ensuring effective prioritization, and signs of habits which would transfer well to the new role.)
- "Give me an example of a time when you had to sacrifice accuracy for speed. What was this like for you?"
- "What do you do to keep track of all the things that require your attention?"

The purpose of the S.E.A.R.C.H. structure is two-fold: 1) to help you create impactful questions for a more objective decision, and 2) to ensure they are behavioral-based questions related to your values and not some random questions you pulled off the internet five minutes before the interview.

## Share The Vision: Outcomes & Responsibilities

The last part of the WHO sCOREcard is designed to create a vision for what outcomes and objectives a successful candidate will achieve if they are hired. Writing down three to five major outcomes and responsibilities the candidate will take on is not just about describing workload. Turn each outcome into a specific, measurable, achievable, relevant and time-bound (S.M.A.R.T.) goal that the candidate can see and respond to.

Interview questions can explore how candidates see themselves serving these goals if hired. Sharing these in the interview allows the candidate to respond to and prepare for success in the role if they are hired. The interview is actually part of the onboarding process. By casting an effective vision and inviting applicants to engage with these goals, you set them up to be activated successfully and build a foundation for effective accountability and development over the whole term of their employment with your organization.

## Sample Outcomes & S.M.A.R.T Goals

### Sample Outcomes for a Clinical Nurse Manager

- Improve patient flow in the clinic and increase customer satisfaction numbers.
- Recruit new team members as needed and improve team engagement.
- Decrease the need for doctors to call your boss.
- Decrease clinic overtime costs.

### Outcomes converted to S.M.A.R.T Goals

- Improve patient flow in the clinic and increase customer satisfaction numbers by ten percent in year one.
- Recruit new team members as needed and improve team engagement by ten percent in year one.
- Decrease the need for doctors to call your boss and earn their trust in the first six months.
- Decrease clinic overtime cost to less than forty hours per pay period by the end of ninety days.

### Sample Outcomes for an Information Securities Analyst

- Systematically evaluate our data storage system for weaknesses or vulnerabilities to new/emerging threats.
- Oversee implementation of pertinent security training for staff members to ensure mastery of our process.

### Outcomes converted to S.M.A.R.T Goals

- Develop a plan to evaluate data storage systems for weaknesses and deliver it within ninety days of onboarding for review with the team.
- Oversee all team members' completion of a security competency questionnaire within the first thirty days.
- Set up learning cohorts for future training and development of staff to ensure participation in security processes appropriate to each role and schedule at least one training within sixty days of start.

## Sample Outcomes for a Sales/Business Development Director

- Develop sales scripts to open new business both over the phone and through social media and email contact.
- Create a top 100 target list of new prospects to target in the first twelve months.
- Implement a direct mail and email marketing campaign to our current customer base.

### Outcomes converted to S.M.A.R.T Goals

- Develop split-test ready sales scripts (A and B) and implement them in at least forty interactions each to sample effectiveness in the first ninety days.
- Target top 100 list conversion of five percent or more into buyers in the first nine months and twelve to fifteen percent by email months.
- Direct mail and email campaigns increase purchasing from our current customers by five percent or more in the first twelve months.

Supporting objectives can add depth to your hiring picture, and allow for nuance around multifaceted roles. These kinds of objectives are clear conceptions of key steps that are needed in order for the candidate to successfully meet the major outcomes. Shoot for 3-8 short- and long-term supporting objectives to flesh out the big picture outcomes.

Some of the core competencies you're looking for will show up as you ask candidates the previous questions. But before you get to the interview stage, do the planning step of identifying as many role-based competencies as you think are appropriate to describe the behavior needed to achieve the desired outcomes. Also include core competencies needed to achieve a cultural fit within the organization (things like efficiency, honesty, customer service mentality, high speed, spiritual openness, etc.)

You'd be surprised how many leaders we've helped in hiring who had no idea what they wanted beyond the job title. Once we've helped them create the WHO sCOREcard they have the clarity to create excitement in the right candidates and repel the ones who aren't a strong fit. Strong candidates want to know what you expect, weak candidates hope you don't know.

## Take Action:

This tactic is all about helping your organization more clearly visualize and be prepared to attract the best new talent to fill your team's roster well. Wherever you are in your organization, there is something you can do to implement or support gaining clarity around new hires. Here are some action steps as examples. Use them as a springboard to imagine more ways to help improve your team's success in hunting for great talent, clarifying core competencies, and embodying your organization's values.

### If You're on the Frontline:

- Identify your own core competencies and practice demonstrating, deepening, and expressing them in your current role. This will serve your current employer and increase your readiness for future opportunities that require these core competencies.

- Identify your company's core values. Brainstorm ways that you could let those values influence the way you go about your work. Let the company values shape your decisions, and seek feedback on how you can do that effectively from your leader.

### If You're a Manager or Supervisor:

- Practice *sapere vedere* from your seat on the team. (Learn more about *sapere vedere* on Pages _____.) Engage in hindsight, look for insights, and practice foresight regarding the company's values and how well your team is living them out.

- Download the blueprint to create your own WHO sCOREcard from **HarbourResources.com** for an important role on your team that you want to fill. Talk to your leaders about getting a competency-based picture of what is needed to really succeed in this role.

**If You're an Executive Leader:**

- Take an honest look at what your stated company values are and practice *sapere vedere* around how your organization is doing.

- Honestly evaluate the pressures and expectations you have set for managers and employees as to whether they are "too busy" to build effective blueprints for talent acquisition. The freedom to prioritize leadership practices like a WHO sCOREcard to improve your organization's hiring must come from the top.

## Extended Resources

If you want a print-friendly WHO sCOREcard template, reach out to my team online. We also offer downloadable reference guides which define Core Competencies and provide extensive sample interview questions like those offered in this section. In the tens of thousands of interviews I have personally conducted, I know the quality and balance of questions asked has determined the success of identifying the right talent quickly. Visit **HarbourResources.com** to download these guides to jumpstart your success in your next interview.

# Attraction Tactic #3:
## *Sharpen Your Job Ads*

Stop copying and pasting.

Most companies who are struggling to get strong new employees are using the same, overworked job ads that have been in the "hiring file" for a decade. You weren't sure it was any good the first time it was used, and time has not improved it.

Using an old job ad isn't always lazy. We'd like to imagine we can leverage "established wisdom" to get a solid result. But more often than not, the people in charge of listing job openings don't have adequate or up-to-date training in how to attract and qualify talent. So, they "use what we've always used" in an attempt to not make rookie mistakes.

But those old job ads aren't attracting the right people and hiring managers blame Human Resources, when in reality the leader needs to help craft the job ad with the use of the WHO sCOREcard.

New applicants are part of the mobile workforce. They refuse to be managed by paycheck. When they start job hunting, they want to see more than a boilerplate job requirement and salary before they bring their skills to your company. They need to see potential for themselves peering out from between the lines of that job ad.

If you're a large company, or growing so much that your team will do frequent hiring in the next five years, strengthening your job marketing will pay dividends repeatedly. But if you're a small team, hiring only one or two people in the coming year, then your hiring choice is even more critical. Small teams mean that each employee has a major impact on company culture, team productivity, and overall success. Spend the time to get that hire right on the front end and the dividends you reap will be just as large as (and often more deeply felt than) those reaped by large teams.

Improvements made in your job ads make quality copying and pasting possible for the future. But every team I've worked with in the past decade has needed to improve what they've got "in the drawer" for hiring occasions.

## Your Job Ad: Part of Your Employment Brand

If you missed Attraction Tactic #1, now is a good time to review what a difference your employment brand makes for the talent attraction process. Think of a job ad like the light bulb you switch on when a job opportunity becomes available at your company. You can buy fancy light bulbs, change them every day, and none of the effort matters if you don't have enough electricity flowing through the power grid.

Whether you know you have one or not, your company has a brand as an employer. When it comes time to bring in new talent, it's the clarity, quality, and strength of your employment brand that influences your candidate pool. Who you are as an employer sends power into the lightbulb of your job ad, making you a brilliant beacon to talent if it's strong, but failing to make an impact if it's weak or broken.

A successful job ad in today's talent marketplace conveys important information about the focus and drive of your company culture, what kind of skills and values will be honored and developed there, and what avenues for growth and advancement can be available to employees who give their best effort.

A great job ad speaks to the heart of what your candidates want for themselves, and shows you're a company where they can earn and enjoy that value.

Building even a single job ad gives you the opportunity to take a look at your company's employment brand. When you flesh out that ad, you can think of it as building a house for the prospective employee to come live in if they get hired by your company. Some elements of the job ad have to speak to the specific role that you're filling. But other elements are part of the larger structure of your company's work environment.

These bigger pieces can be transferred into the job ads for other roles as well.

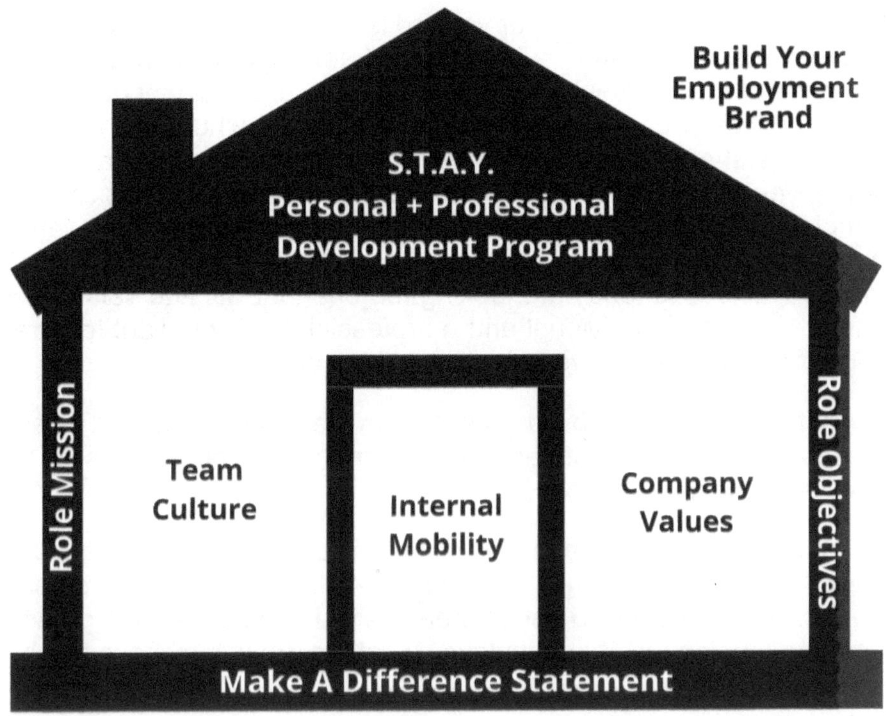


If you worked on your company's employment brand in Attraction Tactic #1, you can use a lot of that work, sharpening the focus for the specific job and creating a powerful job ad with it.

The foundation of your job ad is your Make A Difference, or M.A.D., Statement. Start by bringing into focus the difference your company seeks to make in the marketplace and the world, and you will trigger intrinsically motivated candidates to see the value in working with you. Intrinsic motivation is pure gold in any employee, call it forward with your ad and you will have a better chance of finding candidates who will be more engaged and self-motivated if hired.

The main structure of the ad is formed by the Mission and Objectives of the role you want to fill. This is where you take the clarity you gained from crafting a WHO sCOREcard and put the mission and objectives in terms that speak to the person who would want to apply for the job. What most companies do is list the education and experience requirements, or just describe the duties of the role. But there is a world of difference between casting a vision for what the role accomplishes and listing the tasks to be done by the person hired.

The top of the structure for your ad is formed by sharing the S.T.A.Y. Development Program (review this in Retention Tactic #2). But for the purpose of this ad, think of the personal and professional development opportunities your company offers to the person who takes this role as providing shelter from the elements, making a secure place for the employee to keep growing and thriving if you hire them. This creates an employee value proposition that is bigger than the paycheck, and will bring you better quality candidates regardless of the competition you have. Employees today are looking for jobs that will add value back to them, both as an individual and a professional. If you want to attract a higher quality of employee, don't skip this part.

But like when you build your employment brand, this ad needs to paint a picture of mobility and advancement. We think of this as being the "door" on the job "house."

But most of our job ads paint a picture of static opportunity. Our ad says "come do this work." It sounds like a dead end. Most companies with excess turnover do not provide internal mobility and job growth for existing employees. If an employee wants to grow, they have to job hop to do it.

Keep the talent and knowledge of your employees at your company by offering internal advancement and mobility for future growth. Share that opportunity in the job ad and extend the shelf life of your next hire. If they come into the job with the hope of advancement and understanding of possibilities, they will bring an entirely different approach from day one onward.

And lastly, let your ad reveal your team culture and company values. This should show through in all the other elements of the job ad, but make sure you've been clear. Certain attitudes, mindsets, and behaviors are needed in a candidate who will thrive in and contribute positively to the team culture. Paint a picture of what that looks like so your ideal candidate sees what a good fit they might be.

Every company is different, and each role you're hiring for has unique demands that your job ad needs to serve. What follows are some examples of how a company could use this blueprint to create Talent Attraction Ads for a variety of roles.

# Sample Talent Attraction Ads

## Role: Medical Unit Secretary

Join the North Hills Hospital System and give compassionate care to expand the healthspan of every member of our community. Our mission is to have every hospital admission, outpatient interaction, and home healthcare visit contribute to each patient thriving longer and experiencing better quality of life within the health challenges they face.

As a medical unit secretary, your mission is to build communication pathways between patients and care providers, and to strengthen the accuracy and organization of information in our systems so that the many team members interacting with a patient can efficiently access relevant information and provide compassionate care. The success of our interdisciplinary team's ability to provide effective, health-improving care to patients depends on their access to relevant-information about a patient that paints an up-to-date picture of the patient's status and challenges.

Critical thinking and empathetic communication skills as well as thoroughness and attention to detail characterize the employees who thrive in this role. Passing on questions and conflicts in patient data to the appropriate care team member allows our team to resolve inaccuracies and more clearly address patient issues.

Our culture is one of intentional communication, radical ownership, and collaborative problem solving. North Hills cares about extending the healthspan of every employee, just as we do with patients.

### Perks:

Incentives and advancement opportunities within the North Hills Hospital System will give you room to grow as you gain experience with our collaborative care model. Personal and professional development opportunities are part of the training model from orientation through the entirety of your time with us. Let us know what your experience and ambitions are so we can offer you the best role to grow in.

## Role: Dental Practice Manager

Robinson Family Dentistry specializes in serving patients with special and complex needs, supporting them and their families in receiving oral healthcare. Oral health is a foundational piece of the health puzzle, yet children with physical, social, developmental, and sensory disabilities can find getting oral care terrifying. Come join us in our mission to provide a calming environment with insightful accommodations to make oral care as accessible to children and their families as possible.

Are you an experienced healthcare practice manager looking to make a difference for families with challenges? We need your empathy, skill at maintaining practice management systems, and heart to help each patient receive excellent care. Scheduling and patient flow management is complex as we seek to serve the whole family.

We work to live our company values of kindness, individuality, and possibility in order to create a good experience for employees and customers alike.

### Perks:

Our practice seeks to stay up to date with technology, workflow systems, and new strategies to deliver the best care. Ongoing education, training, and support is part of how we equip every member of our team.

## Role: Regional Sales Director

Coleson Data super-sizes small business competitive data access to reduce risk and safeguard innovation for small companies. Large companies can write off losses in pursuit of innovation, whereas small businesses risk losing solvency. At Coleson, we believe our communities thrive when small companies innovate to serve customers in the global market.

Come join us in safeguarding the success of, and fast-tracking innovation for, small businesses by transforming data into actionable strategies for our clients. Our data solutions are innovative and agile so our teams are always offering the best and most compelling solutions in the marketplace to businesses who need it most.

As a regional sales director, you will support a team with niche territories. Leadership and talent development skills, including the ability to coach and mentor your team, will be key to success. A successful regional sales director will also develop relationships to open new territories and build teams to support the customers in new regions. Foster insight sharing, systematize processes to increase team efficiency, and energize your team with support and accountability.

Our company values include compassionate candor, future thinking, and aggressive learning. You will thrive here if you can acknowledge your own errors, challenge colleagues with respect, and collaboratively work to serve clients in a teamwork environment.

A remote teamwork environment means proactive communication and effective use of networked resources will be key to success. Become part of the network of continuous learning at Coleson Data, where you can sell with confidence in our ability to deliver agile strategies to customers who need our solutions most.

## Keep the Essentials Essential

If I've seen it once, I've seen it a hundred times, overblown ads filled with idealized requirements. What started as an honest job ad balloons into a casting call for a unicorn. Sure, you want to get the best candidate you can. Experience, training, interdisciplinary insights, extracurricular education. These elements might contribute to the strength and depth the employee might bring to the role. But these "nice to have" qualifications can be discovered in an effective interview. They may help you break ties when you've received more qualified responses than you need to fill the position.

Imagine that. Having multiple great options to pick from for the role you need filled rather than getting another warm body in place to carry the workload! But part of being able to collect a lot of good options comes from avoiding the false filter that unicorn job ads put on the résumés you get.

What is really essential for the candidate to have in order to start strong and learn well at your company? Carve that down to a precise blueprint and use it to collect a solid pool of options for deeper inspection. Many great potential employees will have some element of training or experience to gain, and by allowing them to learn and grow at your organization you are enriching talent in a way that boosts your return on that hiring investment. It can also keep your costs down to hire for essentials if there's reason to believe you can train them in missing skills or experience on the job.

This is doubly true if you don't have an endless Human Resources budget. Make sure your job ad doesn't eliminate employees with a great attitude, heart for your values, and adequate skills. Work with those employees and they will shine.

One final question to consider: is the education you often list in a job ad or job description and the years of experience really more important than the person who fits your culture and wants to grow?

I used to be a recruiter, and companies would often say "we need somebody with a master's degree and five years of experience." But when they have a shortage of candidates, I notice that they have left a whole list of candidates who have the required experience, but lack the degree. It's important to challenge assumptions of what is necessary to get strong performers who will be powerful additions to your team culture.

# Take Action:

This tactic is all about creating powerful job ads by zooming out to present a compelling employment brand. Wherever you are in your organization, there is something you can do to impact the way prospective new talent views and connects with your organization. Here are some action steps as examples. Use them as a springboard to imagine more ways to help your organization become an employer of choice where talent thrives.

**If You're on the Frontline:**

- Reflect on your Team Culture & Company Values and ask how you're engaging that culture as an employee, and demonstrating that to others.

- If you have an opportunity to help interview or interact with hiring prospects, think of some questions you could ask or stories you could share to help the employee see if they would thrive here.

**If You're a Manager or Supervisor:**

- Do what you can to honestly evaluate your current job ad copy. Ask yourself, "do we need to completely throw out the old version? Can we intelligently crop and develop it?"

- Review your WHO sCOREcard to bring your target candidate into focus. Translate the employer-centric elements of the WHO sCOREcard into employee-centric descriptions of what it means for the employee candidates. That's the key difference between your WHO sCOREcard and your job ad.

**If You're an Executive Leader:**

- Have you created a strong Employee Value Proposition by offering personal and professional development opportunities within the structure of your organization?

- Does your company have a Make A Difference Statement designed to captivate and inspire intrinsically motivated candidates to pick you over other employers? Do you inspire achievers by showing a greater cause and opportunity for growth or advancement within the role or with mobility to others?

# Attraction Tactic #4:
## *Interview as a Team*

Team interviews sound like a time-consuming logistics nightmare, right? Maybe you figure team interviews are an option for teams that aren't too overloaded. That they're something you can wait to do until after you get the essential roles filled.

But team interviews aren't a luxury; they're the difference-maker if you want to win talent and develop a power culture in your organization. Done well, team interviews eliminate some of the costliest forms of turnover—employees who should never have been hired in the first place. I see this all the time. Companies lose ninety days of onboarding (plus all the time wasted in interviews) waiting for the chance to let go of someone people sensed wasn't a good fit even before the offer was made.

Why didn't those people speak up? Why let the team suffer through disqualifying the new hire and start the hiring process all over again? Quite simply, the people with insights were not asked, or their attempts to be heard about it were not listened to.

Often, clarity about a potential candidate's inadequacy comes from a variety of perspectives. Especially if your company uses a hiring team to evaluate candidates, the people they will work with are left out of the vetting process.

It isn't your altitude on the organizational ladder that gives you wisdom about whether a candidate is a good choice for the job. So let's get some of those perspectives in on the interview process and cut the dead weight of bad hiring choices.

# Reduce Bad Hiring Choices with Deep Perspective

Having other team members in on the interview gives depth to your perspective on how strong the candidate is. Even if the primary manager who could handle an interview solo is experienced, they are limited by their perspective, their role, and their life experience. The more diverse roles and perspectives you can get at the table, the broader your insight will be on the potential new hire. This includes noticing strengths, potential, weaknesses, and warning signs.

Gain this perspective by preparing team members with some ideas of what to look for, as well as letting them know you'll want their general sense of how the new candidate could struggle or thrive if they were hired. If you've created the WHO sCOREcard together then you've won half the battle to prepare.

When I say diversity, I don't mean giving a surface sense of visual diversity by asking people to "sit in" for appearances. I mean reaching to multiple levels on the hierarchy, and crossing departmental silos to get diversity of thought, priority, and experience. Look above and below the level of the position you're hiring for; you may be shocked what these individuals pick up that just didn't hit your radar.

As a leader, you'll need to weigh the perspectives and investigate red flags or doubts further. In the end, as a leader it lands on your desk to make the call one way or another. This is not hiring by committee. But by listening to other team members, your judgment will have more source material to work with as you weigh the decision about the candidate.

## Build Credibility by Listening

There's another huge payoff from asking team members to give perspective on new hires. Doing this values and engages your existing employees' input. Every spot on the roster comes with insights that can enrich your leadership. But most leaders and managers don't take the time or make the effort to gather this kind of input. When you listen, you are valuing your employees in a way each worker needs to thrive.

The number one reason people make job changes today is because of their direct supervisor. Sometimes it's because they don't know how to give praise, communicate well, or they play office politics. But if I had to sum up the majority of explanations for why a good employee leaves a company it's "because I'm not valued here." Team interviews improve your attraction power. They also turn the tide of disengagement by valuing employee's input and honoring their perspective.

## How to Save Everyone's Time

Just because someone has a good résumé, it doesn't mean they're a good candidate for your team. And just because someone has a bad résumé, it doesn't mean they're a bad candidate. Unfortunately, many companies screen résumés, and then conduct in person interviews with the key managers or team members present. This often means some strong candidates are screened out, even though a quick interview would have shown they have a lot to offer that didn't appear in their résumé. It also means the hiring team wastes time in interviews with people who aren't even close to a fit for the culture just because they made it through their résumé screen. How many hours have you spent in interviews with people who you knew in the first fifteen minutes were not a fit for your company?

This is why I teach companies to create a brief (fifteen minute) pre-interview screening call that can be handled by Human Resources (or just one member of the hiring team) to get a preliminary sense of a prospect's fit with the culture. Let the team create a small set of screening questions the screening interviewer asks every promising résumé candidate. If they get enough good answers, they can schedule a more thorough interview with the hiring team.

You can also save time by including some key questions about the interviewee's readiness to join your team in the more in-depth interview. If you like a candidate in a more thorough interview, tell them "You seem to have a lot of strengths that would be an asset to our team. If we were to offer you the position here, what would be in the way of you saying yes to it? Any barriers or questions you would have before you would be excited to accept?"

You'd be surprised how much time these tactics save, leaving you room to conduct team interviews with the right prospects. One of our clients, Infinity Health, has saved thousands of dollars and countless hours of time by implementing the screening interview. Employ it yourself and your quality of hires will reflect that strategic time investment.

## Who To Include on a Hiring Interview

When you're picking your interview team, go deep and wide. Going deep means pulling from multiple levels in the hierarchy. From managers, all the way to the frontline. Going wide means crossing department lines. Silos are deadly, whether it's the invisible line between sales and service, the no-man's land dividing management and workers, or cliques between departments with their competing budgets and deadlines.

More often than not, your new hire's success will depend on them being able to interact successfully across the organizational silos to get information, cooperation, and support from others. Build buy-in on the new hire from the people who will be responsible for their success by including those people in the team interview.

Team members who helped in hiring an employee often feel a sense of ownership in the new employee's success down the road. If they're going to object to the new hire, better for those objections to be identified and addressed before hiring happens, or they may sabotage the success of the new employee. Quality objections often lead to calibrating the onboarding process to overcome deficiencies or diffuse problems before they derail the success of the new hire.

To be sure, team interviews don't guarantee that everyone will magically agree on who is the best candidate. Like I've said before: a team interview is not hiring by committee. But involving the team in the process makes it possible to address, deal with, train, prepare for, and resolve friction and potential talent killers proactively. Expect to learn from the voices you take into the interview room with you.

Participation in the team interview process does more than smooth out the onboarding process, and improve your perspective by getting a variety of insights before hiring someone. It also builds trust, rapport, and the skills of future leaders on the team. By preparing and involving an employee in the interview process, you are investing in the skills they'll need when they become leaders down the road.

The goal when hiring is to always uplevel the quality of performance on your team. Don't replace a poor employee with another poor employee. This can happen when you just connect the dots based on the job description of the last employee in the role. TAGS (an acronym for Task, Accomplishment, Gain, Sustain) helps us keep our goals and values on track for growth with new hires.

# TAGS Interview Method

### Task

What experience do you have doing tasks which must be done well in this new role?

### Achievement

What was the result created by the actions you took?

### Gain

What value was created by the result?

### Sustain

How did you contribute to continued gains and growth in this gain?

## Use the TAGS Method to Assess Functional Competencies

The TAGS method is a competency-based (sometimes called behavioral-based) interview technique used to gather relevant information about a specific capability that the job requires. Using questions, explore how the candidate completed a Task through to Accomplishment, what Gain that brought their team or organization, and how they participated in Sustaining that gain to let value continue to develop over time.

Choose job- and team-relevant tasks and ask interviewees to give examples of how they have handled similar tasks in previous settings. Seeing this provides clarity for the interviewee about the demands of the job, and invites them to share examples of relevant experience they have in delivering on similar demands in the past. This interview tactic allows you to better predict future on-the-job performance than the traditional interview, which usually has surface level questions that fail to challenge the candidate or the interviewer.

Remember to include the interview team members in identifying the most essential tasks you will use the TAGS method to investigate.

The idea is to rise above checking boxes about people's listed skills and education, and get a real picture of how their experience will transfer to the role you are considering them for at your company. Just going down a list of requirements may result in a warm body hire, but are you getting someone who can help your company create real value and amplify that value over time? TAGS will help you find candidates who can. Using this tool in conjunction with what you created in the S.E.A.R.C.H. questions will take your interview objectivity to a whole next level.

## Score Using an Interview Matrix

Once we have the key tasks in mind, and questions ready to explore candidate competencies, we need a clear, quick way to visualize the assessment each interview team member makes of the candidate. If you don't have a way to do this objectively, team interviews result in an unnecessarily long round table discussion of "how did we like this candidate?" With a scoring matrix, you paint a clear picture of objective scoring that each interview member can fill out individually. Let each team member run their own tally and report an overall score, or crunch the numbers in a spreadsheet to coordinate data from larger teams or longer interview processes.

To do this effectively, you will lay out the core competencies (including task mastery, areas of experience, and embodiment of values) to fill one column. Then give a weight (or importance level) to the score of how important each competency is relative to the others, and leave an empty blank for the score to be given on the day of the interview. Some interview teams plan ahead which team members will ask questions about each competency.

A sample interview scoring matrix could look like this:

**Interview Scoring Matrix**

| Core Competency | Score | | Weight | | Total | Comments |
|---|---|---|---|---|---|---|
| Analytical Skills | 4 | x | 3 | = | 12 | Gave multiple examples. Able to DO. |
| Empathetic Communication | 3 | x | 3 | = | 9 | Average, seems competent. |
| Systems Thinking | 4 | x | 1 | = | 4 | Outshines other candidates on this. |
| Proactive Accountabiliy | 1 | x | 2 | = | 2 | Seemed to not prioritize this value. |
| Collaborative Teamwork | 5 | x | 3 | = | 15 | Very experienced. Able to TEACH. |
| Customer Service Skills | 2 | x | 3 | = | 6 | Could use training, but adequate. |
| | | | | **Total:** | 48 | |

Interviewer experience can massively influence our sense of the candidate and overshadow objective considerations. Even if unconscious bias doesn't play a role, there are simply a lot of factors involved in the candidate being successful once hired. Use a scoring matrix to avoid hiring errors brought on by fatigue, distraction, unpreparedness, or bias. It will help you more objectively evaluate how candidates stack up against one another.

When doing team interviews, the interview matrix allows you to objectively aggregate the insights of the diverse team you have evaluating the candidates. This saves you the time and hassle of getting subjectively "unanimous" selection of a candidate. It also gives interviewers signposts for investigating further what a team member may have scored someone poorly on. Instead of asking "why did you not like this candidate" you can ask "I noticed your score for this candidate's core competency in communication skills was low. Could you share a little of what tipped you off to this?"

## Building Your Matrix

As shown in the sample matrix, keep track of candidate responses during an interview with a pre-planned matrix grid. Pre-print or create a digital scoring matrix for each candidate before starting the interview. Using a digital matrix can make aggregating scores easier, especially if you're interviewing an extensive list of candidates, or have multi-site interview teams.

Whether analog or digital, be sure to include a scoring key to remind interviewers of what each weight and score is intended to mean.

For example:

Weights (1-3)

1 = Preferred, but not necessary
2 = Moderately Necessary
3 = Essential


Scoring (1-5):

1 = Answer not reflective of questions asked. No experience or example was provided, and skills are not evident.

2 = Limited experience or example(s) shared. Satisfactorily answered but with little depth. Will require additional training.

3 = Specific examples and experiences shared. Not all actions ended in the desired result.

4 = Solid experience and supported examples shared. **Can DO.**

5 = In-depth experience and example shared. **Can TEACH others to do.**


Some hiring managers will choose to set the weight of each core competency ahead of time. In these situations, the interview team will offer diversity in their perspective of how well the candidates showed their competencies. But some hiring managers will ask their interview team to set the weight of each core competency from their perspective. This can deepen the perspective that is gathered, and provide helpful conversations within the team about prioritization. Noticing large differences in the priority of the various core competencies can be a warning signal that different members of the team perceive the role differently. Mismatch in priority can cause trouble in the onboarding process, especially if multiple team members are involved in preparing and training the new hire.

Perhaps most often, the praise our scoring matrix approach receives is that this tool drastically reduces the time it takes to gather input from your team. Ten team members can report their scores and offer insight on why they gave pertinent scores in a few minutes, contrasted with the time it takes to package and explain your perception of the candidate if you don't have a structure to use. Because it becomes quick, we can reliably hear from all the voices at the table, rather than missing insights when we inevitably run out of time for unstructured feedback.

## Reducing Unconscious Bias

Many of us are tempted to skip this section, thinking we have dealt with our biases. But there's more to bias than obvious preferential treatment of someone. We all have unconscious biases that creep in. They can include enthusiasm for sports, fitness, conservation and more, or modes of self-expression including tattoos, piercings, or clothing style. Even political and personal choices, such as masking behavior, can set us up as for or against candidates unconsciously. An unconscious bias could be the assumption that younger candidates will be less dependable, or older candidates will be harder to train.

Subjective interviewing cannot protect us from bias, but objective interviewing can. Implementing a clear interview matrix into your process can help to create a more equitable environment and help you see through the barriers that biases would create.

There are a lot of great reasons to create more equitable, fair workplaces. Our workplaces have an important role in fostering social justice and equality. But in the hiring setting we reap rewards that go beyond fairness. Increasing the diversity of thought, experience, and perspective makes our workplaces more creative, resilient, and innovative.

Using pre-defined screening questions, creating a clear WHO sCOREcard, planning the interview ahead of time, and using an objective scoring matrix can help eliminate unconscious bias to create a more equitable interview process. Without something concrete and fair to measure applicants against, hiring can be a "gut decision" that makes managers vulnerable to unintentional bias.

This unconscious bias is why workplaces grow homogenous, favoring and preferring candidates who look, sound, or seem to be "more like us." The self-fulfilling prophecy that says "all the best candidates I've ever hired were this way" may operate on a skewed sample of experiences.

We instinctively trust our experience. But if we surround ourselves with others who have the same experience, we lose that essential diversity of thought our teams will need to solve problems, innovate, and become wildly successful. Get more people in the room, and like many lights together can eliminate shadows, multiple perspectives will help us see beyond our own limitations.

## Role Play for Success

Most leaders never do enough hiring to become true experts at hiring through trial and error. Even if you could get in your ten thousand hours, as Malcolm Gladwell coined, to become an expert, you wouldn't want to. Hiring is important, but it's only one part of what you need to become great at. How can you bypass trial and error to start having stronger interview experiences right now? Run role play interviews. A role play interview lets you practice asking the questions you plan to use with real candidates with other members of the interview team.

Most professionals who haven't done this resist. Role playing sounds awkward. Unfortunately, the alternative to pushing through the awkwardness of practice is an awkward or ineffective interview. If we experiment our way toward good questions during the interview, it means we're not getting a strong interview with all of our candidates. What if the first interview you have scheduled is the strongest candidate you'll see? If you don't have your questions calibrated before you start, you may fail to uncover their gifts.

Experimental questioning also can leave room for unconscious bias in interviewing. Asking questions to some candidates and not others can create an inaccurate picture of a candidate's strength compared to their competitors. We don't even know when we offer this inequitable interview experience because subtle shifts subconsciously cause us to offer a very different interview from one candidate to the next.

Get a list of expert interview questions and choose a few that you think will help you discover what you need to learn about your candidates. Then team up with someone on your team to practice asking and answering them. If you rarely interview, run a few practice sessions to get multiple perspectives on the questions. Time invested to massage and clarify your interview questions will bear dividends in the speed, equality, and effectiveness of your time with every candidate you interview.

## Prepare Your Team to be Part of the Interview

Including team members in the interview can display positive culture to candidates, and draw them to want to be part of your team. Prepare employees to share their perspective of what it's like to work at your company and with the current leadership team with the candidate. From their perspective, what is valued here? How could a candidate prepare to be successful here? Who would thrive? What are the challenges here? Work with team members to help them recognize this is not a time to offer vague "it's great here" propaganda, but a time where they can give some specific ideas about what new hires can expect.

But what if you don't have a positive culture yet? Working with team members to equip them to participate in the interview process can help you turn the tide. It can also clarify areas where culture development needs attention and warn you of future problems that need to be addressed.

If you struggle to identify who could give positive "here's what it's like to work here" input in an interview, that's a warning sign about your team's quality of life and engagement. Are you uncertain about how disgruntled employees are, or certain they are disgruntled? Either way, that's a priority problem to address.

> **Reality Check**: Whether you have team members in on the interview with you or not, they will eventually convey their perspective on how it is to work at this company. You can avoid having them interact with the new hire during the interview process; but at some point the dissatisfaction of any employee begins to infect the rest of the team.

Where appropriate, include the interviewing team members in choosing which core competencies to prioritize. Let the diverse group of voices you're bringing in have a say in suggesting which skills or values are paramount, and invite their input on setting the weight for each skill. Even a cooperative, positive group of people may not agree completely. That's not detrimental. By listening to the input, you as the leader will have more clarity in finalizing the interview matrix. Expect to learn from the voices you are bringing to the table.

The team you involve needs to be prepared. They should know exactly what questions they're asking and why they're asking them. They should understand how to use the scoring matrix and why. This preparation is key to having great interviews and providing a great experience for the candidate.

DO NOT ask five or ten people who are unprepared and only create negative energy in the room to join you in a group interview fifteen minutes beforehand. This is disrespectful to the candidate and to your outcomes. Then you will say the process doesn't work.

## A Note on Canned Questions:

It's a great idea to use pre-written questions from experts as a starting place for crafting interview questions. Most managers can instantly improve their results just by borrowing better questions from a qualified professional. But ALWAYS take time to tweak and customize the questions to really help you discover whether the candidate matches what you're looking for in skills, culture, and values. Take those questions out of the box, and sharpen them well.

# Take Action:

This tactic is all about turning a time-consuming, siloed hiring process into an efficient, objective, team-based process that sets up the entire lifecycle of talent at your organization. Wherever you are in your company, there is something you can do to help generate insights, and promote the successful selection (and elimination) of new talent for your team. Here are some action steps as examples. Use them as a springboard to imagine more ways to help your company become a talent attraction magnet.

### If You're on the Frontline:
- Reflect on what you notice in the team culture that's contributing to (or detracting from) the company's ability to draw and keep talent.

Be prepared to give constructive feedback when the opportunity to speak arises.

- The next time someone is a potential new hire, see what you can do to pass on your insights for how to be successful and thrive in your current team culture.

**If You're a Manager or Supervisor:**

- Ask your employees what they like about working here? What do they like about working with you specifically? What do they like working with the team? If you're concerned you won't get good answers, or you know people will react negatively, get curious and clear about what's wrong. Addressing this will never get easier, so start today.

- Rise above your feelings of time pressure. Make space to prepare yourself and your team to do interviews with intention. Ninety-nine percent of the hiring mistakes I've witnessed could have been eliminated if the manager had spent even fifteen more minutes preparing, rather than rushing into an interview unprepared.

**If You're an Executive Leader:**

- Make room in your organization for improved interview processes. If your company isn't using screening interviews, get that time-saving system in place. If your team isn't using team interviews, make space and time for your staff to begin implementing this to improve the quality of your hires.

- Look at the homogeneity of your teams. Where are you lacking diversity of thought and depth of insight? Your current system is the cause of what you have now. It will not improve on its own. What changes will you make as a leader that shift the course of your company for the decade to come?

**Extended Resources**

For downloadable templates for resources described in this chapter, visit **HarbourResources.com**. You don't have to reinvent the wheel; just start using one that works, today!

# Attraction Tactic #5:
## *Close the Deal or Close the Loop*

Each piece of the talent attraction process is important. Without a clear vision of who you need and an effective way to evaluate prospects, you're at the mercy of the next warm body to walk in your door. But figuring out what you need is only half the battle. You've got to be able to close the deal. Done right, the interview initiates the onboarding of new talent in a way that draws the best version of them into the workplace, setting the tone for their entire tenure with you.

For too long we have treated disengagement as a cleanup problem, and one we blame the employee for, when in fact we fail to provide an engageable workplace for the talent that comes to us. Engagement levels have been abysmal for decades. As low as twenty-five percent of employees reported feeling engaged at work in 2005. Even the slight improvements seen in the past few years (hitting a high of thirty-six percent in 2020) have shifted backwards. In 2022, positive engagement levels had dropped to thirty-two percent for a representative sample in the US, with active disengagement levels as high as eighteen percent.[35]

Many leaders don't realize that the way you close the deal in an interview can significantly raise engagement levels.

## See the Candidate

There's a lot you can do to improve your interviewing savvy, but none of it matters if you don't realize your primary job is to really see the candidate—to both see them and make them feel seen. Some of the talent warming your conference room chairs won't make it through the hiring process to join your team. But even these candidates provide an opportunity to strengthen the attraction power your company has.

Your plate is full, I get it. You'll have to make an effort to unhook from the regular grind of your duties and make space to see these strangers trying out for a spot on your team. Make or borrow some form of interviewing agenda, and set expectations for yourself that help you arrive in the right headspace to identify the hidden gems and catch the warning signs waiting in your applicant queue.

Sure, if there's a brilliant candidate practically glowing with perfection waiting in your pile, you'll probably see they're awesome even if you rush in unprepared. For those candidates, your ability to make them pick your company hinges on your preparation. But the glowing candidate has options. They don't need you as much as you need them.

Being prepared and making up your mind to really see each candidate means that you may help a talented applicant who is nervous or quiet to share their skills with you. Creating a comfortable space, sharing a bit about yourself and what you love about working at the company, and demonstrating genuine interest in the candidate turns the light up so candidates shine back at you.

The same is true with candidates who lack the experience or knowledge you need on your team. If you fail to dig into their experience, these candidates can signal a lot of the right answers without having real knowledge to back it up. Take a little time here, and you've saved yourself weeks of wasted time on a bad hire.

Previous tactics such as creating the WHO sCOREcard and Interviewing as a Team are powerful tools for helping you really see the candidates who walk in the door and getting a strong sense of what they can offer the company in that role.

## Inspire Engagement

When you develop your company's "Make a Difference" statement (see Attraction Tactic #2), you are bringing into focus some of the meaning of working at this company. The job interview is not a lecture or deep dive course on company propaganda. But you do yourself and the candidate a huge disservice if you fail to paint a picture of the vision and meaning embodied by your team and the company as a whole.

Build on the company's MAD Statement by sharing some of how the big vision shows up in your day-to-day workload. Connect the dots to share how the role the candidate is interviewing for is crucial to helping the team make a difference in specific ways.

Human beings have a switch inside that flips when we see a chance to make a difference. Being fulfilled at work, knowing the day's efforts mattered, those are things people today are searching for. With burnout at an all-time high, if you can show that this role makes a meaningful impact on the company, you signal to your future employees that this is a place where they can give their full engagement and know it will be valued.

## Say No

But even if you offer the best pitch in the world to the most awesome list of applicants, you won't want everybody. Most of your interviews will end in a "no thank you." Don't mess up with the no candidates; they are a huge part of your employment branding.

When you're overworked and overscheduled, it can be tempting to do nothing once you eliminate a candidate. Let them realize when they don't get a call back that they didn't get the job. Don't do this. The law of reciprocation says that we get what we give. Is it any wonder we're getting ghosted by interviewees, and having ghost hires? Be a pro! Let them know when you know they're not going to be a fit.

Have you ever had a candidate waste your time "thinking" when they already know they don't want the job because they don't have the courage to tell you? You're not a prom date; it doesn't make it easier on you to hold out hope that will be eventually dashed anyway. If they know they're going in a different direction, an honest, unhesitating communication of that fact will save you time and cause you to respect them more.

Give that same respect to your interviewees. It is a considerate thing to do, but that isn't the only reason to do it. So much of your employment brand is built by people who don't currently work for you. Ex-employees and rejected candidates go back out into the hiring pool and talk to others about their experience with you. They get hired at other companies but take their memories of the interview with your team with them. Even top-notch candidates are worn out by the process of applying, interviewing, and waiting for news that never comes. Help them close the loop. Become an employer they wish had said yes to, an employer they have something positive to say about, and who they would consider in the future when a better fitting opportunity with you comes up.

Best practice demands more than an email message. Pick up the phone, or plan for a real human from Human Resources to deliver the "no" to the talent in a way that reinforces the worthiness of your employment brand. Even if you tell the candidate "No," they can become a positive force for building your reputation as an employer of choice with the candidates out there that you really do want.

## Show Your Cards & Check for Barriers

If you've used your Who sCOREcard and interview scoring matrix to evaluate candidates, you get a pretty clear picture during an interview of whether a candidate is a real, strong possibility for the position. Even if you can't say "definitely this person" yet, you often know before the interview is over that you may want to offer them the job. Sensing they're going to make the short list means you have an opportunity to lay the groundwork for closing the deal. You do this by making it clear, before you even get off the phone or leave the conference table that you see them as having a lot to offer the team.

I'm not sure what kind of power play we have been trained to make. Old school ideas of "keeping them guessing" and not telegraphing your interest seem to have entered standard hiring practice for a lot of companies. Hiding our interest allows uncertainty to remain for the candidate, making them feel the need to hedge their bets. It also prevents us from getting a clear sense of barriers that might already exist on their end.

Here are four questions you can use with candidates who have potential to be your next great hire. They show your cards, which allows your prospect to do the same.

> "It seems like you have a lot to offer a team like ours. If we were to offer you the position, are there any barriers that would keep you from saying yes?"

"You're clearly qualified for the position. It is essential for our team to fill this position well and as swiftly as possible. The right candidate for us would be someone who could begin immediately. Is there anything that would prevent you from starting right away if we did offer you the position?"

"Thank you for interviewing with us. We'd love to have you on our team. If we offer you this job, would you be able to say yes and set a firm start date?"

Is there anything you feel the need to wait for at your old job, or any resistance from a partner or kids that could prevent you from being excited to relocate or start working here?"

Don't be shocked by barriers that pop up in between the interview and getting a real yes. They're often there, so make a habit to always check for barriers. Barriers exist to protect us. You won't have success getting a real picture of the actual barriers if you don't make the candidate feel safe by showing your cards first.

If you remain vague and non-committal, your candidate won't feel safe to forthrightly warn you of their barriers. This isn't because they're sneaky; it's because as the leader it's your responsibility to create safety and clarity in the situation.

Some hiring managers act as if revealing we like candidates will drive up the price of getting them to work with us. This mindset treats your employees like an expense you're trying to minimize, rather than an asset you're trying to acquire in top working condition. And at the end of the day, in my extensive experience helping teams hire talent, the thing that drives up the cost of acquiring talent tends to be the negative vibes new employees receive, not the positive ones. Think of it like a culture tax. If an employee knows right from the interview process that positive feedback and energy are in short supply, they will need top dollar pay to compensate for the undesirable work environment.

Give them a preview of a positive culture right from the interview, and back it up with a culture generous with praise and appreciation, and you will reduce the cost of your human assets by keeping them longer and inspiring engagement. This part of the interview is a preview of your leadership style. Can you create trust and openness or do you create doubts?

## Start Onboarding Immediately

I know I'm repeating myself, but I've got to say it again: The interview process is the first step of onboarding. Engagement levels, readiness for accountability, and communication patterns begin to form the instant the candidate starts interacting with you.

This is why leaders who fly into interviews unprepared spend months cleaning up bad hires or retraining new employees who didn't get started right. Often the responsiveness, honesty, and clarity that is needed to hold high performers accountable never gets established if it's not established at the beginning. The interview is the beginning.

Checking for barriers to beginning work is one of the things that reduces slow or unsuccessful hiring. Build on this by sharing the goals and objectives you have, and some of the strategy for what success looks like in this role, during the interview. Then ask the candidate for questions they have about what it looks like to succeed in their new role.

Don't wait for the onboarding process to begin. By getting them engaged in the expectations and vision for their new role now, you allow the candidate to more adequately prepare themselves for success when onboarding starts.

## Share Your Why as a Leader

People don't choose a job. They choose a workplace. They can get a job anywhere to earn money. Day to day, they don't work for a company as much as they work for their direct manager, or supervisor, and their coworkers. Their leader sets the tone for their experience of the company culture.

If you're that leader, you are a huge part of why someone will stay or go, work hard or punch the clock. People defy management by paycheck. They won't work hard for you just because they're "supposed to."

But there is something you can do to spark intrinsic motivation and enthusiasm in prospective new hires. You can share what your deep motivation is—share your **Why**.

Why do you do what you do? What is meaningful to you about your work, the customers you serve, the culture you're helping create, the products or services you're helping create and deliver to customers? Why are you leading a team instead of simply handling a workload?

Sharing your motivation is a way of inviting the candidate to bring their own motivation to their job. By opening up this way, you also demonstrate trustworthiness and authenticity. In order to have an honest interview, onboard and upskill a new hire adequately, and help them reach their full potential, you will need vulnerability and honesty from them. Mistakes, performance dips, and growth opportunities all require that the people you're leading feel safe enough to admit not knowing something, and don't feel threatened when they receive critical feedback. Part of how good leaders create psychological safety at work is by fostering a sense of meaning and value. By connecting their own personal vision to the vision of the organization they work at, leaders help to create a healthy culture.

## The Leader's Reality Check

The push to share your **Why** during the hiring process can be a wakeup call for leaders. How deep do we have to dig to find our own emotional connection to the work we do every day? Does it feel false, stiff, or strange to say "the reason I love coming to work is…" because we don't love coming to work anymore?

Any client who has worked with me knows I'm not someone who lets my emotions keep me from staying focused on reaching my vision. But I understand that I need to discover and connect to my own **why** at work in order to lead with authenticity. If I don't love coming to work, I need to address that inner conflict.

This reality check can extend further, sometimes further than we're comfortable with. What happens if you as the leader are responsible for several hires that didn't pan out well? Maybe you've reached for this book because you're tired of going back to square one and hoping the new hire this time will be more motivated, more engaged than the last few. If that's you, remember, motivated people gravitate toward workplaces with motivated leaders.

Do the tough work of dealing with your own disconnect at work if necessary. But when the time comes to interview new talent, get ready to show (not just tell) why it's great to be part of this team.

## What to Include in Your Why:

Your **Why** statement is going to be as unique as you are. But here are some strong elements you can consider including when you craft yours.

## Competitive Advantage:

What you think makes this company different from other companies shows their competitive advantage. Personalize this as part of your **Why** by explaining why this difference is meaningful to you as an individual.

## Personal Values:

What are your top workplace priorities that are honored here? Do you prize autonomy, clear guidelines, industry leadership, social impact? Do you value working here because a certain skill is appreciated, or things are done in a specific way?

## Work History:

No interviewee needs to hear your professional life story. But consider including facts of your work history that help your prospects get a sense of your perspective. If you've done something in the past that makes you value the work you do here, share that.

Some leaders get really good at sharing their Why in just a couple sentences. It takes practice, but when you do this, you become someone who can more easily connect with your colleagues.

Many people don't like to think of themselves as a salesperson. For some odd reason many of us have been conditioned to see sales as slimy. The reality is, every day we are always trying to sell ideas to others. It could be a spouse, a child, friend, coworker or boss. Maybe it's the cop who pulled you over for speeding and you're trying to sell your way out of his ticket.

I want to challenge you to see selling as influence. And just like leadership, we're attempting to influence someone to buy our idea, position or leadership. When you are interviewing, you are influencing others. Your personal Why is the greatest motivating piece of the interview. People buy into the leader before they buy into the job. If they don't like you, then the decision is only about money. If they see how you connect to your role as a leader, it allows them to connect to your leadership. People are motivated by a leader who knows why they lead.


# Take Action:

This tactic is all about how to close the deal with new talent for your team. Wherever you are in your organization, there is something you can do to strengthen your organization's employment brand, get a clear sense of whether a candidate is a good fit for your team, and actually get the right applicants in the door to start working with you. Here are some action steps as examples. Use them as a springboard to imagine more ways to become the place employees truly love earning their paycheck.

**If You're on the Frontline:**
- If there is a job opening on your team, think about what insights you have on what would make the next employee in that role even more successful than the previous one. Look for an opportunity to contribute to the new person's success by giving your input if asked.

- Connect yourself to the Make a Difference Statement your company has. If they don't have one, make up one for yourself by describing in words that are meaningful to you, what difference you make from your role every day. Live into this to reduce your own burnout.

**If You're a Manager or Supervisor:**
- Notice the difference between the "job requirements" usually listed in a job ad and the values and core competencies that are essential to the success a new employee would have with you. Be prepared to investigate values and competencies rather than just asking questions about interviewees' résumés.

- Think about your Why as a leader. Why do you do what you do—supervising, leading, or training others—rather than working in a non-leadership role? Reconnect with your Why if it has grown distant.

**If You're an Executive Leader:**

- Set an expectation for how your hiring teams handle rejection of applicants. Being allowed time to say "no and thank you" has to come from the top.

- Assess your hiring team's 30-day and 12-month turnover rates. Teach your hiring teams to show their cards, and prepare candidates for accountability as demonstrated in this section to reverse this kind of turnover.

## Extended Resources

If you need an interviewing agenda or printable resource to help you prepare for effective interviews, visit **HarbourResources.com** or contact our team. A simple tool can help you focus energy where it's effective in the midst of your busy work life.

# Activation: Launch Their Potential Quickly



When I was young, I joined the Army. Onboarding came in the form of eight weeks of sweat and exhaustion. Boot camp activated my potential to handle life in the military. Later as I was ready for promotion to a leadership role, I had to go to eight weeks of Primary Leadership Development Course (PLDC) to unlock my leadership potential.

At every phase of my military career, I passed through an activation process to prime my ability to succeed and reach mastery in my new role or duties. While boot camp and PLDC provided what I call in business "universal training pathways" that every person goes through at the appropriate level, other activation processes like Army Individual Training (AIT) provided the "individual development plan" to prepare me for a unique position on the unit I was headed to. In my case, AIT consisted of a year where I was prepared to be a specific kind of medic, using my skills as a physical therapy assistant in my military position. AIT looked different for me than it did for other soldiers headed for different roles.

In the military, you don't get promoted by punching a clock and watching the calendar lose pages. I had to keep learning, take courses, and demonstrate mastery of what I was being taught in order to earn the advancement of a new title or elevated responsibility.

The same should be true for the employees in your organization. Everyone gets a cohesive basis from the universal training pathways in onboarding, initiating them into the culture and vision of the organization. Then each employee should move continuously through the individualized training and equipping steps that allow their talent to continue expanding as they fulfill their potential inside your organization.

How different is the process at your company? Are employees expected to magically become better without a clear and strategic pathway for obtaining and building the mastery they need to be successful? Are they thrown in the line of fire to work without solidifying their tactical skills and building defenses against the challenges they'll be asked to handle?

# Costs of Failing to Activate

Sift through piles of résumés, interview a football team's worth of candidates, and you can still bring on a new employee who struggles to meet productivity for an entire year. You may even hire someone in good faith and have them quit showing up in their first week of work. Does this mean the wrong person was hired? Not necessarily.

Something crucial happens to every successful employee. Their potential gets activated. We will share some activation ideas to follow during the interview and after the job has been accepted. In the first days and weeks of a new hire's tenure at your organization, they have the potential to connect and engage with your culture, processes, and productivity flow. But often all, or part, of this engagement fails to launch.

In dramatic cases, new employees feel lost in the new environment, struggle to learn, and give up on the job, within thirty to ninety days, before training is complete. This hard bounce is brutal for morale, and costly to your overhead. But at many companies, the new hire fumbles through an uncomfortable first year. The costs to productivity for poorly initiated team members follow them long term.

## Cost #1: New Hire Bounce Rate Increases

An effective S.T.A.Y. Process keeps talent with us sixty-nine percent longer. From a talent perspective, the bounce rate at companies should be looked at in three metrics: The first thirty days, ninety days, and twelve months.

If we've lost them within the first thirty days, it's a failure of the interview. If they're lost in the first ninety days, we didn't do an adequate job in the onboarding process; their talent didn't get activated well enough to fuse into and engage the work and culture. If they make it past ninety days, but bounce within the first year, it's often a sign that the support and development they received during onboarding dried up once they shifted from "new" to "staff."

## Cost #2: Drain on Team Efficiency

Failed onboarding kills productivity. Anytime current team members have to pick up the slack for an underperforming employee, the team loses traction and the leader loses credibility. The risk of losing a good employee or two because of the inequitable workload caused by a poorly initiated new hire goes up dramatically. In this case, the leader often blames the new employee; but the rest of the team sees the failure for what it is—a failure of leadership. Even if they show frustration toward the new employee, they're looking at the leader to solve the workflow issues.

It isn't that the leader is necessarily the one training the new employee. But they must lead existing employees in helping the new hire gain mastery if it's ever going to happen.

If you're reading this and you're not in the leadership role, let this be some validation and a caution to not "fake it 'til you make it" when you're learning a new process or taking on a new role. Whether you're changing jobs or taking on new responsibilities where you've worked a long time, get the help you need to learn so you don't burn yourself out.

## Cost #3 Rookie Mistakes Get Perpetuated

The longer we wait to solve training issues, the longer mistakes happen. Many leaders blame the employee, when the system of activation needs to be addressed.

If you are in healthcare, this could mean life or death for the customer. A famous, and challenged study by the National Institute of Health in 2017 identified over 250,000 preventable mistakes each year in the American healthcare system.[37] But an even more conservative estimate from current research claims "Preventable adverse events in the United States of America (US) cause an estimated 44,000 to 98,000 deaths in hospitals each year."[38] Consider if you or one of your family members ended up harmed by a mistake which could have been prevented by better onboarding.

Without proper onboarding, rookie mistakes get perpetuated. That's not okay. The employee may no longer be new, but they're still making rookie mistakes months or years later. Scarier still, these poorly-activated employees will pass on habits, attitudes, and information to new hires, duplicating their deficiencies indefinitely.

# Create a S.T.A.Y. Development Process

In the Retention section of this book, we introduce the concept of a S.T.A.Y. Program as one of the talent magnets you can embed in your company. People want to work at a place where they know they'll be seen as individuals and helped to grow and achieve. That S.T.A.Y. Process is launched by activating the new hire's potential immediately following a successful interview. While the term onboarding is most common, I will continue to refer to your company's "S.T.A.Y. Process" because it's the kind of onboarding that creates a talent lock that lasts into the future and is sustainable.

According to some sources, a good onboarding program leads to sixty-nine percent of employees staying at least three years.[11] When combined with other employee development strategies, those numbers get even better.

Get new talent activated, and you'll reap dividends for years to come. Fail to fully transfer your culture, your processes, and your team dynamics and new talent will bring in theirs—good or bad.

What we usually think of onboarding is often no more than a hit-and-run orientation (park here not there, don't do this with your timesheets) and paperwork checklist. Onboard people right and they will stay and grow as long as they are with you; fail to do so and you've just started the clock on another employee turnover in progress.

I have worked with organizations that do this well, but they are few and far between. Many organizations have become so hyper focused on adding a warm body to fill a need that they don't even consider how onboarding the warm body from the interview process forward impacts retention. Solving your challenges to retention of good talent begins in the S.T.A.Y. process.

How we do anything is how we do everything. Shortchanging a new employee at the start will lead to blame and excuses in other areas. Create a robust S.T.A.Y. process, execute on it, and watch your team thrive.

# Activation Tactic #1:
## *Master the Welcome*

Once someone makes it through the screening and interview process, they enter a phase of initiation at our company. Even if a prospective employee takes the job we've offered them, there's still a chance that they will quit showing up without warning. Often this kind of failure to launch can be avoided with strategic welcome processes. They start long before the employee's start date, extending back as far as the successful interview. The goal is to get them excited to show up because they know they will be appreciated and valued as an individual.

To give an example of what an effective welcome process can look like, take the example of one of my clients who built one for his healthcare team. Let's call him Alex.

Alex's team has been looking for a new administrative assistant for one of the busiest departments in the organization. Once hired, the new employee will report directly to Alex. Alex participated in the team interview for the candidates, and worked with the interview team to select the strongest candidate.

At the end of the second interview, the candidate was verbally offered, and accepted the position. Alex opened his drawer and wrote a quick card welcoming the successful candidate to the team, thanking them for bringing great energy to the interview process, and dropped in the mail immediately.

Alex then scheduled check-in reminders to touch base weekly leading up to the new employee's start date. If the new employee starts immediately, then at least three days before they are set to start with the company, Alex will call to ask if they've got any questions or concerns, make sure they know where to park, and where to enter the building, and make a plan to meet when the new employee arrives.

On their first day, Alex walks out to meet the new employee at the entrance, and escorts them in to help them feel welcome and make sure they don't get lost. As he leads the new employee in, he makes introductions to staff members along the way, and points out some of the key resources and locations on the property.

Alex isn't the primary trainer for this new employee, so he blocks an hour toward the end of the employee's first shift to check in, answer questions, and address any issues that have come up.

## Keep the Talent Warm

In our example, Alex doesn't let the talent get cold feet between saying "yes" and starting work. At many companies, the talent acquisition process includes several weeks of dead time between a candidate's acceptance of the position and their first day. Whether they are giving notice or relocating, the waiting period between your interactions in the interview and the start of onboarding is a high-risk time. When the employee gets disconnected during this period they may fail to show up for training. This hard bounce can often be prevented if we build connection with the employee during the wait, rather than letting their enthusiasm and engagement go cold.

Even if all you need is a warm body, you still need to eliminate the turnover of quick talent loss. But if you need real talent at your organization, then this means **engagement** needs to be your priority. Getting another person on the payroll does nothing for your company if you're not activating the drive and productive passion of your new hire.

Check in with new hires weekly leading up to their start date. If they are putting in two weeks notice this could be two check-ins. If they have vacation time to use up, a project to finish, or a life transition period, this could be eight weeks or more.

Check in weekly with that new employee.

These check-ins can be phone calls, texts, emails, or even hand written notes. Aim for answering questions, hearing feedback from the new employee, and keeping your ear open for barriers or confusion that might become obvious while you wait. This is also a good time to get to know more about your new employee's strengths and personal goals.

If you anticipate a long wait, you may want to plan a strategic connection point, asking for example if the new employee would be open to completing a strengths or communication styles assessment so that you can prepare to lead and support them in an individual way.

## Sample Check-ins:

- Welcome note thanking them for choosing your team, and letting them know their new colleagues are excited to have their talent and energy come join the team. Consider inviting the team to sign the card.

- Phone call to verify they've been in touch with HR and gotten their questions answered about the logistics, benefits, or other details involved in getting started.

- Barrier check: follow up on anything uncovered in the interview that could slow down or derail the transition. For example: needing to find a replacement for their current employer, finding housing in the area, or finishing a necessary training or certification required before starting.

- Logistics check: call to discuss how they will navigate either their first day virtually or onsite. Describe where to park or how to log on, and make plans to connect when they arrive onsite or online. Don't underestimate the impact "showing up" to help them navigate the virtual environment can have in remote workplaces.

- Confirm they have resigned by checking on how it went and if there are any new challenges their current employer has added to the mix.

- Offering direct access by email or mobile number, as appropriate, to help with problem solving or to reach your leader if anything comes up.

- Introduction email to connect the new employee with a peer mentor or team member to answer questions or virtual shadow to help them know what to expect.

- Personally check what name they want to go by and set for their company email address. Rather than letting IT set these facts from their legal information, the leader can ask "what would you like to go by." People's names are important; don't miss the chance to build positive energy.

As you look at this list, the principle that becomes apparent is that a leader who activates the talent of a new hire looks for things they can do that allow increased contact with the employee they plan to lead. Directions on where to park, assigning an email prefix, and even confirming start dates can all be handled by automations and other staff members in various departments; but letting other people handle these things doesn't increase your connection and relationship capital with the employee you are hiring.

So have that chat about what they want their name listed in the employee directory, and then pass that on to HR for implementation. Don't let efficiency steal the small moments where you can make big changes in the team dynamic with the new person you are bringing onto your team.

## We Don't Have Time to Hold People's Hands

Wait. I know what you're thinking. None of us have time to spoon feed unmotivated employees. You want to find talent for your team who are self-motivated, ready to learn, and actively engaged in making things happen.

But don't forget how disorienting a new workplace is. A paycheck is nice, but most of your workforce wants more than to be treated like an interchangeable body, doing a job like a puppet. They need to feel like they matter and that they have a place to be recognized and valued for what they do. They will experience less friction, wasted time, and social awkwardness if they have a little help finding their way around from the very beginning.

The notes, phone calls, and personal guidance into the office for the first time (or virtual welcomes and tours for remote onboarding) are your ways of investing in the new employee as a person. It builds a bridge of positive regard and communication that is key for noticing and fixing talent-killing issues before they become barriers.

Think of this process like cultivating your garden. The fruit you want to harvest ninety days in the future must be planted, nurtured, and tended to before you're rewarded.

## Don't Kill Engagement with Poor Email Habits

Email is one of the primary ways most leaders and supervisors interact with their direct reports today. Even if you're not in a remote workplace, email is essential for communication. Unfortunately, leaders can forget that email isn't just about conveying information. The tone and content of your email messages has a relentless impact on your colleagues' perspective of you. Daily clues to whether you appreciate them, are actually listening, or are responsive and supportive of them being able to get their work done, come through in these small messages.

As a leader, you've got to go beyond email etiquette and excuses. If you take responsibility for the impact your email habits have on your employees' engagement levels, you will be making a daily difference.

This starts with your welcome email. When someone new joins the team, you have an opportunity to start fresh, cultivate positive energy, and set the tone for long-term success.

Studies tell us that fifty percent of employees won't even read an email from the CEO. And of the fifty percent of employees who open that CEO's email, fifty percent of them will merely scan the content, rather than reading. At the time of this writing, the latest numbers available showed that up to seventy-one percent of employees don't even read company emails at all.[40] What is email but a minefield of unnecessary information mixed with messy action items? Email can be a major part of an employee's anxiety paradigm. Change how you handle email or your employees' inboxes will become the graveyard where your most convenient mode of communication goes to die. Avoid these common pitfalls when you start communicating with your new employees.

1.  **Don't Get Right to Business:**

If the first messages you fire off to a new employee are task-oriented emails, you are training them to skim and defer email until when they can deal with tasks. Even if your team is operating at a dead run, take time first to welcome the new team member as a human. They're the new talent joining your team; they're more than the project you're working on right now, more than the tasks that need to be done. People need to be valued first, before they can give their best value back. Set a conversational tone with new employees so email becomes a conversation that doesn't get tuned out.

**2.  Don't Send Group Welcome Emails:**

If multiple people are joining your team at once, it's tempting to create a group welcome email to save time. Group welcome emails tend to do more harm than good. Why? Because they teach the new hires to view emails from you as blasts and chatter. The welcome email should be a moment of direct connection, offered in their inbox as a way to communicate with you. Group welcomes turn you into a loudspeaker; over time loudspeakers are tuned out. If this is happening to you now, strategize ways to bring more individual connections to your email "voice." We want to teach our new hires that our messages matter. Poorly targeted emails don't prime our employees to open our messages; they promote scanning and low response rates.

**3.  Don't Make Excuses:**

Even fabulous leaders have weaknesses. It's important to be aware of these areas and work on them. Unfortunately, the onboarding process can become a time of excuse-making disguised as orientation. Leaders say "I'm bad at email," or "I sometimes forget to send stuff after a meeting, so you just have to keep reminding me," or my "just text me if you haven't heard from me and it's urgent." That's not orientation; that's asking a new employee to enable your flaws. Maybe the system you have isn't working, or you could work with a coach to untangle the block to your workflow. Keep doing the work to grow yourself. You are the leader. Don't ask your employees to pick up your slack.

## 4.  Don't Fuel Burnout with Constant Connectivity

If you send emails at odd hours, this can drastically increase burnout for your employees. Even a boss who "doesn't expect an immediate response" is still polluting the employee's off time with an unresolved ping. The sense of "emails waiting for me" increases any workday dread they feel. Too many of our employees have anxiety, and this adds to it.

If you do expect them to answer out of the office, wait. Your employees have personal lives that should matter more to you than getting a response to your email right away.

Email whenever you want and still respect an employee's quality of life by scheduling the email to deliver during work hours. Protect your employee's "off the clock" hours even if you find it necessary to draft a message during your personal time.

The more messages sent at times when you "don't expect a response" the more your employees have to learn to tune out your email messages. Do you really want them to do that?

Also, remember email is **a** tool; it's not **the** tool.


## S.T.A.Y. Welcome Timeline

If you're a visual person, here's a summary of the kind of onboarding welcome that initiates the S.T.A.Y. Development Process. This process is designed to create a talent lock for your company.

**STAY Welcome Timeline**

| Pre-Activation | |
|---|---|
| 1 | Schedule Weekly Check-ins Leading Up to the Start Date |
| 2 | Plan To Welcome Them Personally (Virtually or In Person) |
| 3 | Call Right Before Their First Day to Confirm & Coordinate. |
| 4 | Set Up & Prepare a STAY Navigator for Training & Guidance. |

Consider the day an offer is made and accepted as the start of the pre-activation period. This starts the countdown to a strong onboarding process. Immediately mail the new employee a welcome card or gift.

Thank them for a great interview, and let them know you're excited to have them on the team.

Speed the new hire through the pre-onboarding process with HR as much as possible. Make sure the new hire doesn't lose momentum in the slog of drug screenings, background checks, paperwork, or preliminaries required by your company. Help them get a jump on this by playing an active role in turning them over to the HR process.

As you move forward in a new hire's onboarding process, you'll get to support and hold them accountable to become a productive, high-achieving team member. But in order to do that smoothly and efficiently, each new employee needs to start well in the physical or virtual environment.

If you don't have an established welcome process at your organization you risk losing time every day to the new hire's struggle to find their rhythm. Feeling connected to someone right from the start helps the new employee hang in through the confusion that inevitably makes starting a new job exhausting. Many of the rapid turnovers companies have each year could be avoided with this foundation of connection to help the new hire survive the chaos of getting started.

## STAY Welcome Timeline

**Activation: Day 1-30**

1. Meet Them At the Door (Virtual Welcome If Remote)

2. Accompany / Escort them to their Work Area and Introduce the Team

3. Show Intention With a Lunch Order or Treat on Day 2

4. Schedule Weekly 15-minute check ins for their first 90 days

5. Assign a Preceptor, Trainor, or Mentor (STAY Navigator)

6. Set 30-, 60-, and 90-day Progress Reviews

7. Praise the Efforts and Energy they Invest in Growth, Productivity, and Becoming Part of the Team

The principles this activation schedule presents are ways that you can intentionally participate in helping each new employee feel seen, appreciated, and listened to. In order to do that, first day greetings aren't meant to be convenient for you—they are meant to happen the moment the new employee arrives. Acts of hospitality and warmth like ordering the employee's favorite lunch and eating with them if possible, or preparing some sort of treat for the team in the new employee's honor are meant to be specific to the new employee. So get to know them during the Pre-Activation check-ins to pave the way for this. Using a tool like our QLT Employee Engagement Profile Card is a great way to create this individual value.

It also means that the weekly check-ins to monitor their progress, and the thirty-, sixty-, and ninety-day reviews are not boxes to check where you ask skill-oriented questions. These are meant to be two-way accountability conversations. During the interview and onboarding process, promises are made to the employee. They're told what they're expected to do, and what kind of support they will receive.

Every check-in with your employee should involve some version of the question "how are we doing on our promises to you?" Talent stays with companies where people feel seen, and where their grievances and struggles are met with respect and willingness to improve.

## Onboard Agency & Contract Staff

If you are in healthcare, use temporary staffing, or employ contractors to handle part of your workload, onboarding can be completely forgotten. Who signs the paycheck is the least important thing about the employee working with your company. Most customers won't even know these employees are not "official employees." What matters is their ability to become a productive and connected employee for whatever hours they are with you.

How can an employee advance your mission, transmit your culture, and fulfill the real demands of your organization's vision if you don't effectively transfer your culture and values to them? Rushing an agency nurse onto the floor to start their shift is not caring for productivity. Your patients and other staff members will pay a price if this nurse is not pulled into the culture of the team before being set free to do their work.

One of the biggest benefits to "onboarding" temporary staff is that it reduces the strain and friction caused to your permanent team.

Employees resent outside talent popping in to gain higher pay while being asked to do fewer of the things that contribute to long term systems and consistency on the team.

Onboarding temporary staff can look like a fifteen-minute check-in to prime the employee for the team's focus and priorities as well as touching base on the competencies you need to verify are up to speed with the employee. It's in your best interest to give the same attention to the training and competency of temporary staff as you have to full-time staff.

If contractors contribute to your team's projects, don't let them stay aloof. Make strategic plans to onboard them to your culture, even if you are not their only employer. Making the work that contractor does rewarding, engaging, and meaningful means you get the best out of that employee and their efforts are more fully in sync with the culture and rhythms of their colleagues within the organization.

If you do this right. you can actually recruit them to join your team when they decide it's time to stop doing contract work and become part of a team full time. They will choose the leader and company that respected and valued them the most and helped them grow even in a temporary role. And if they stay independent, they will still become part of your team and culture.

## Onboard for Promotions & Role Change

The last kind of onboarding that is often missed is the kind that needs to happen anytime someone experiences internal mobility or a change in responsibilities. A talent lock comes from implementing a S.T.A.Y. Development Process that doesn't end when the average concept of "onboarding" does.

Every time things shift for your employee's domain of work, it's an opportunity for their talent to be activated! Management experts talk about how a learning organization is one that continuously and systematically elevates the assets of their team's skill, knowledge, and collective productivity with learning and mastery. Personal mastery in particular requires the input and challenge that comes from new opportunities combined with adequate training and feedback.

I see it happen every day: an experienced employee is asked to take on tasks or responsibilities outside of their original training with the organization. But rather than receiving any clear training, they receive the assignment and are left to figure it out for themselves. How would you train someone new to the organization to handle that responsibility? That's what you need to give the internal hire.

**Slow is smooth and smooth is fast.**

I've trained and conditioned my mind and body for many challenges. From the US Army's boot camp, to hiking the Grand Canyon with my son, I learned that the only way to stay with something long enough to conquer a great challenge is to build like there is a tomorrow.

You would be shocked by what fifteen to forty-five minutes of microlearning can do to activate your team's talent. Don't cut corners because your employee has other experience at your company.

Promoting an employee from a technical role into a management or leadership role is another space where companies miss the mark every day. Just because someone has mastery of a skill or process doesn't mean they have the communication or people development skills to transfer that knowledge, hold people accountable, or activate the talent of others. **Activate** the next leader you promote, don't expect them to simply know how to fill the new role the way your company most needs.

# Take Action:

This tactic is all about actively connecting to new employees in a way that activates their talent. Wherever you are in your organization, there is something you can do to make people feel seen and valued, and contribute to them reaching mastery faster so that the entire team benefits. Here are some action steps as examples. Use them as a springboard to imagine more ways to help talent dive into your culture and start pulling with the team.

### If You're on the Frontline:
- Reflect on your own training and onboarding experience. Are there processes that you struggle with or skills that feel squishy? Reach

out for help achieving mastery so that you can be more engaged and feel energized at work.

- Notice your inbox experience. Is there a productive conversation you could have with team members about improving the communication style? Do you need to have a conversation to clarify expectations about email responsiveness at work?

**If You're a Manager or Supervisor:**

- Identify the kinds of emails you send (consolidated/discrete), and check your send times. Have a conversation with colleagues and direct reports about what kind of messaging would better support their focus and productivity.

- Broaden your perspective to notice opportunities to activate the talent you are responsible for—new employees, transitioning employees, employees with changing responsibilities. Make time to coach and mentor to help your employees' mastery and teamwork rise.

**If You're an Executive Leader:**

- Prepare to peel back the automaticity of the "onboarding" process and develop a S.T.A.Y. Program that systematically makes new employees feel like an individual.

- Set expectations and space for managers and supervisors to participate in welcoming new staff. If you want your employees to mature like the assets they are, model and implement the welcoming of talent to the team.

**Extended Resources**

Visit **HarbourResources.com** to download a free onboarding worksheet.

# Activation Tactic #2:
## *Structure 90 Days of Onboarding*

Onboarding is one of those activities we can do that improves all of our tomorrows. Pains and potential all reflect the early efforts we make in a new team member's experience at our organization.

We throw around words like "welcome" and "onboarding" in our organizations all the time, but we don't always know what makes a welcome effective or an onboarding successful. Just as the previous section laid out some concrete elements that your "welcome" needs, this section will take "onboarding" to a concrete place as well. We will paint the picture of how to prime your new employee to stay with your company long term, and increase in value with every passing season.

Let's start with an ego check. Most companies who are failing due to their poor onboarding processes believe they can't afford the time to improve them. This tends to be an ego problem. Either we think what we do is so complex that it can't be transferred systematically to others, or we think our time is so valuable that we "don't have time to worry about that."

You want them to engage and stay right? You can't afford to fumble activation. There are few things as important and valuable as interrupting business as usual to improve an employee's first ninety days.

Take a step back from the chaos and noise of your workload and think about the long-term impact of getting each new team member started strong. Studies continually show that the first ninety days with you makes or breaks the productivity, profitability, creativity, and longevity of your employees. The first ninety days are the most important days in the new employee's life with you and the leader leading them. It's a time to establish trust, connection, and expectations instead of hoping it happens by chance.

Do this even if you are not the primary leader, or responsible for hiring. If you want your team to flourish and the culture to be energized, look for any ways you can contribute to the effective onboarding of the next new team member. Contributions you make to support them reaching mastery and excellence sooner pay dividends into your work and the overall success of the organization around you. Even if "leader" isn't in your title, you'll be a leader if you do this.

## Don't Hit the Ground Running

Inadequate onboarding systems can create an excess burden on coworkers, and long-term gaps in knowledge for the employee who is asked to "hit the ground running." This common phrase, used by many of us without thinking, may sound like a way of asking the new hire to jump in and give their best. But beware: failing to equip and upskill new employees from the start creates several risks.

If you're hiring anyone now or within the next year, it's a good time to look at your company's onboarding processes. If you've just onboarded new employees, take the opportunity to evaluate how effective the process is, and whether parts of the onboarding process were skipped or seemed outdated. As part of this evaluation, encourage honest feedback about the onboarding process from new hires and other team members. It is easy to blame people for a bad hire, when it could really be a problem with the S.T.A.Y. Process.

Make it clear when asking for feedback that it's the onboarding process itself that they are evaluating, and that their perspective will help you strengthen it going forward. New hires often feel insecure about sounding like they were unhappy with a supervisor or trainer, and don't want to be labeled "a complainer." It can also be hard on the team if they feel they're being asked to criticize or flatter the new hire. Instead, encourage everyone to think about the process itself and help your team notice where the training may have failed or succeeded.

Too often we blame a new employee when they don't hit the ground running. In reality, we should always check the system first.

Criticize the system. Coach the employee. Also, don't make the mistake of thinking an experienced employee can hit the ground running because they have done a similar job before.

If you've been doing without the hires you need for longer than intended, the temptation will be strong to shorten or skip parts of the onboarding process to help them "get to work" faster. Resist the urge; your company stands to benefit exponentially from having new talent masterfully onboarded.

## Equip a S.T.A.Y. Ambassador

Systems continually need feedback and improvement. Sometimes the system is well designed, but the implementation of the system breaks down at the level of the supervisor or leader training the new employee. Even a company with a good onboarding program needs to gather feedback from the new employees to see if they are learning and connecting to the culture. An effective S.T.A.Y. Process requires weekly evaluation to identify and address friction and flaws in activation so that employees reach mastery fully and quickly.

It is this S.T.A.Y. Ambassador who is tasked with assessing whether a new hire's talent is being activated or not. Where are there holes in the equipping? Where are (and aren't) they gaining mastery? Is there early detection of leadership or training issues? If you are responsible for turnover rates or accountable for staffing costs, become the STAY Ambassador for your next employee who onboards.

Schedule weekly check-ins for the first ninety days. This doesn't have to be a laborious process; but if it is intentional, you create a net to catch talent at risk of leaving your organization because of preventable problems that arise in the activation stage.

## Empower a S.T.A.Y. Navigator

Where a S.T.A.Y. Ambassador is someone who checks in on how the process is going at meaningful intervals, the S.T.A.Y. Navigator is someone who takes an integral role in actively training and mentoring the new employee to help them reach mastery in the execution of their work. Many companies assign a peer to help a new employee find their way around, but if this isn't done in an intentional way the peer mentor often fails to activate the new employee's talent.

The three main mistakes companies make when attempting peer mentoring during onboarding are:

1. **They Assign the Employee with the Most Time not the Most Excellence**

   Put your best, most qualified employee in a position to activate the new talent, not the least qualified (and therefore least busy) employee. Your new hire will imprint and perpetuate the habits and processes modeled by the person who shows them the ropes. So let them learn from the best.

   This goes for attitude as well. If you're trying to improve the culture at your organization, trying to curb toxic communication or negative behaviors on the team. Don't pair the new employee with a team member who doesn't embody the positive culture you are trying to create.

2. **They Don't Give the Peer Mentor Notice or Preparation**

   Have you seen it as often as I have? A new employee shows up for their first day, and in the morning meeting they get paired up with someone on the team who had no idea they'd be asked to train them. That person went from trying to manage their own workload to trying to orient someone new. Usually the new employee suffers through awkwardness, and sometimes hostility, as they are now an unexpected inconvenience. Not a great way to get started.

   There are two types of preparation any S.T.A.Y. Navigator needs in order to do a good job transferring the culture and processes to the new employee. They need to be equipped with the appropriate level of people development skills, and they need to be given time to mentally prepare to give their attention to training someone. Just because someone is great at doing the work doesn't mean they have the skills to train someone else. Get them ready, and let them know ahead of time.

3. **They Don't Adjust the Workload Expectations to Allow for Effective Equipping**

Transferring the culture and processes to someone new so they can gain mastery is a high value activity. It takes attention, time, and focus. In order to do this well, adjustments usually need to be made to the workload expectations so that the S.T.A.Y. Navigator doesn't drown in their own workload while they're bringing the other person up to speed.

One of the most common reasons new employees are slow to reach mastery is because they are rushed through orientation processes. Instead they should be given time to learn and do it themselves with the support of the S.T.A.Y. Navigator to help them. Regardless of learning style, full mastery requires being able to do it for yourself. But if the S.T.A.Y. Navigator is in a rush, chances are they will rush the new employee and the training process will break down.

At the end of the day, the more people in your organization who have been taught how to transfer the culture and help their colleagues achieve mastery, the more agile and productive your team will become. Increasing the transfer rate of positive culture and equipping builds a sort of team immunity to fight off the everyday stressors of demanding customers, risky markets, and unexpected changes.

# Onboard for Mastery

Part of human nature is to enjoy being good at things. Often, our team members who are performing poorly have lower job satisfaction. Their job satisfaction scores often improve significantly when they receive the training and coaching they need to become masterful in their work. The confidence of doing what they know is valued, and the satisfaction of completing necessary work masterfully becomes part of the payoff.

When we onboard employees for mastery, we don't have to give pay raises we can't afford or manage workers within an inch of their lives.

Instead, we have employees who know they're valued and are less vulnerable to burnout. They also reduce the cascade of overwork that escalates the burnout of other team members.

When employees aren't getting satisfaction from the work they do, and don't feel like they're effective at work, burnout skyrockets. But what is it about the onboarding process that is so important for creating a sense of mastery?

How you start sets the tone for everything that follows.

Rushing employees through a proper onboarding process, delaying training until "things slow down," and failing to inventory and work through each necessary skill and procedure for doing their job with excellence, means that most employees start work with insecurity, inflated error rates, and unnecessarily elevated stress levels. This leads to burnout and lower performance that can last the entire time they're with a company. In my experience, leaders blame the employee when the system itself needs the upgrade.

Letting new hires slip through the cracks during their onboarding means they're likely to replicate their mistakes and deficiencies in future hires. Rookie mistakes become part of the culture. Simply having more seniority than future hires means that these employees will likely pass on flaws and misunderstood information that could have been corrected in their own onboarding. But once someone isn't new anymore, scrutiny and support for them in acquiring knowledge and mastery is often lost.

The impact of one poorly-onboarded employee boomerangs with each subsequent new hire that they have an influence on. Use a clear checklist of competencies, skills, and processes that the new employee needs to master to move with confidence and high productivity. Defining what "mastery" looks like in the new employee's role makes room for accountability, and provides a focus for training and equipping efforts.

Don't be one of those organizations that doesn't step back to analyze the skills and processes your employees need confidence in and skill with. These might be people skills to go along with their technical know-how, or a short list of processes they need to be able to troubleshoot on their own. Either way, map a ninety-day plan to instruct them and allow for implementation and feedback so that you can verify their ability to do their work well independently.

More often than not, new employees are given a list of core competencies to be trained in, but no time or access to ask for help in problem areas. They may be given leniency for "being new" but they aren't given a navigator or coach to help address the missing pieces so that they solidify personal mastery.

Below is a sample Universal Training Pathway Checklist for a new staff member. This is a basic example and a real checklist would possibly be several pages long to encompass the myriad tasks a new employee would need to learn. Use this sample to get you started.

## Sample UTP Onboarding Checklist for New Staff Member
### Orientation Activities

- Review organization's mission, vision, and values.
- Meet with the organizational leadership team to understand your new role's goals and objectives
- Get access and initial training on data systems and proper use.
- Learn all the keycodes and how to maneuver from department to department.
- Meet with the Department Director to establish S.M.A.R.T. goals for the next six months and review the onboarding checklist.
- Understand call-off process and our expectations

### Core Competencies Development

- Teamwork:
    - Foster a positive work environment and promote collaborative teamwork among the team.
    - Learn our core value of effective communication strategies to ensure clarity and efficiency in working together.
    - Learn our process for strong decision-making, and when to ask for guidance from the team.
- Technical Expertise:
    - Demonstrate up-to-date knowledge of best practices for using each piece of equipment in the department.
    - Learn our regulatory standards and best practices.
    - Embrace our culture of continuous learning and professional development.

- Understand our security policies for all equipment
- Performance Management:
  - Establish two to three S.M.A.R.T. goals around our stocking and replenishment systems to master in the first ninety days.
  - Within the first ninety days, master team member names and who is an expert in each key function.
  - Ask questions to address performance issues promptly and implement improvement strategies.
- Quality Improvement:
  - Collaborate with the quality improvement team to identify areas for improvement.
  - Analyze data and implement evidence-based strategies to enhance outcomes.
  - Monitor and evaluate the effectiveness of quality improvement initiatives.
- Relationship Management:
  - Foster effective relationships with vendors, cross-functional teams, and other departments.
  - Facilitate open communication and collaboration among team members.
  - Learn our customer service model by the end of ninety days.

## Activate Potential at Every Opportunity

While getting a clear and thorough onboarding strategy in place for each role at your company will put you ahead of many companies who are flying by the seat of their pants, there's something that the best companies do to put their onboarding processes in a league of their own. They enrich their onboarding with additional input over time.

As employees execute their work for months and years, the domain of work can drift. In our rapidly changing economy and quickly shifting technological landscape, the skills and processes our top performers are using to do their jobs keeps changing. Because of this, we need to facilitate the dialogue between those who are doing the job, and Human Resources. Great leaders make it possible for input from working team members to enrich the training and onboarding that new hires will receive when they join the company.

While this can mean asking for periodic input from current employees, it also means gaining insights and strategic input from employees who are leaving our companies. Go back and review the Release tactics (or read them if you haven't already) to learn more about that.

But if you are onboarding new staff, help them acquire the most mastery possible by inviting the right input to keep making your onboarding process the best it can be. This also means activating employees who aren't new to the organization every time their role or responsibilities substantially change.

## S.T.A.Y. Development Process

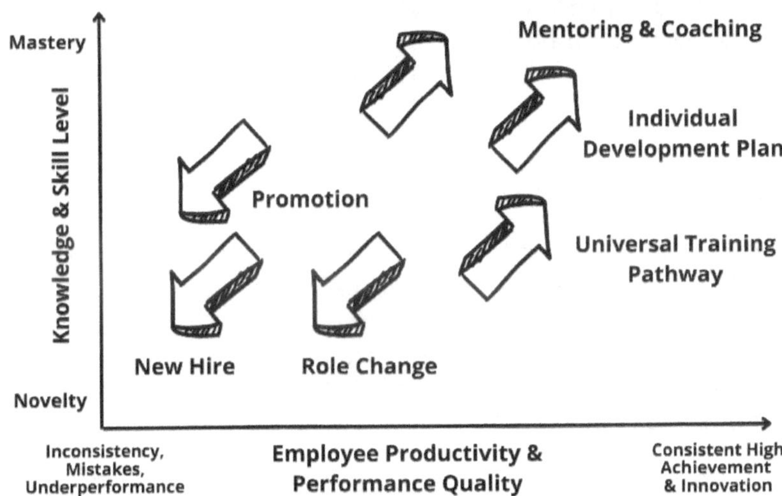


# Twelve Weeks to Mastery

Most talent loss could be avoided by helping new employees achieve personal mastery in their role, and helping them build a sense of connection and belonging in your culture. So instead of "showing the new employee around," get intentional to create a solid twelve weeks of clear learning and competency objectives they will work through with the help of the right members of their new team. This onboarding process is guided by a checklist of all the must-know behaviors and tasks in the department or for the role. It involves moving them through understanding to action and into mastery.

## Pre-Activation

We focus on this in Activation Tactic #1: Master the Welcome. We won't repeat all that here, but remember the focus in these first ninety days isn't checking boxes. It's activating the potential of your new employee. So whatever you do, don't put your new employee in a conference room with a book of company policy or log them into a "learning portal" with nothing on it but outdated onboarding videos about rules and regulations.

Create and review a twelve week plan of learning and competency objectives with the new employee. Explain the kinds of help they will have, and designate the S.T.A.Y. Navigator and/or coach they can confidently ask help from. Establish a schedule of anticipated progress checks where they can plan to ask questions or get feedback to solidify confidence.

## Activation

An activation plan usually features a mix of shadowing, training, and opportunities to execute some of the duties required in the new role at a slower rate and with coaching support. I have yet to meet an employee whose ability to do something well was activated by being dragged at full speed through a never-before-seen process and then left behind to repeat the process solo.

During this period, connecting the new employee to peers and mentors, and supporting the formation of social support is a key goal. If you want your new employee to stay, research shows they need to feel like they have at least one "real friend" at work.[42] Workplaces that incorporate the "buddy system" as early as the onboarding process fast track building resilience in their new employee.

Weeks one through three should include some of their representative workload, but not the full workload. If you are training and coaching them to build connections in the workplace and transferring the company values the way you need to, handling a full workload won't be possible during these first few weeks.

## Mastery

Review the ninety-day plan you created to guide their progress toward mastery. After the first thirty days, an employee in a new role may be handling fifty to seventy-five percent of their full workload. An experienced employee may already be at productivity workload in the first four weeks. Clarify the expectations around workload management, and continue to support the employee in reaching productivity.

Don't make the mistake of thinking onboarding is complete as soon as the employee is at 100% productivity. It's impossible to fully unlock an employee's potential in less than ninety days. If they're already at 100% productivity within thirty days of starting with you, it means they have more potential. Keep supporting them to help them reach full mastery and identify where their potential can be further unlocked to increase the ease, creativity, and energy they experience.

Often, our newest employees push hard to handle their workload to make a good impression, but they are more drained and anxious than they should be because they haven't achieved mastery yet.

Don't just look at workload and productivity to determine how the new employee is doing. Ask them where they feel things are slow, foggy, or stressful. Early on is the most profitable time to deepen skills that increase ease and energy in executing the everyday work on their plate.

Sometimes the employee won't ask for help with clunky processes or confusing workflows because they don't want to complain. But their fresh perspective can provide insight that allows the team to improve flow and efficiency for everyone. We recommend utilizing the five-step equipping formula outlined in Activation Tactic #2.

## Lock In Learning

Each week should end with a short coaching session or training check-in to close the loop on that week's learning and connection objectives. The twelve week S.T.A.Y. Process plan or onboarding learning objectives may look impressive but they are worthless if you don't methodically reconcile progress every week.

Take the time to ask the following questions **every week** and you move from box checking to mastery formation. You will catch costly problems at the moment when you can most easily fix them. This is also how you can earn the trust you'll need from this employee to hold them accountable in the future.

## Weekly S.T.A.Y. Coaching Questions:

1. How well did we honor our commitments to you this week in our training and coaching?

2. How fully did we accomplish this week's goals from the onboarding plan?

3. Where do you need more time or guidance to gain mastery of this week's learning objectives?

4. Did you experience any friction or resistance from team members this week?

5. It's important to me that we create an environment where you feel like you belong and are appreciated, how are we doing on that so far?

6. Will I see you next week?

7. Is there anything that might prevent you from coming back?

Do this and thank them for the way they engaged this week. Let them know you look forward to continuing to learn more about them and helping them be successful in the weeks to come.

As you go week by week, expect to repeat and revisit things taught in earlier weeks. Keep looking for opportunities to help increase mastery (which involves energy, smoothness, and competency), rather than judging an employee as a "good learner" only if they "don't need things repeated."

In school I wasn't a good student. I was horrible at learning math. I needed the lessons to repeat over and over, again and again. But in anatomy and biology courses, I soaked it up like a sponge and still remember many of those things today, even though I've never studied them again. In one area I needed drip learning and in another, you could throw it at me. I was labeled dumb in some of those classes. I wasn't dumb; I just learned those things differently or slower.

With our new employees we need to seek to understand how they learn. We need to adapt and adjust our training plan for their style without calling them dumb, slow, or disinterested. Giving them space to ask and repeat the learning is the sign of a great leader and S.T.A.Y. Process that values them as an individual.

Schedule thirty-, sixty-, and ninety-day coaching sessions to review progress. Spend at least half an hour evaluating their areas of growth and need for additional training. Give praise and express gratitude for efforts and energy they are investing in growing, being productive, and becoming part of the team.

Once the onboarding is completed you should have a highly-productive team member. Shift your weekly coaching to monthly coaching and development sessions to help them achieve the goals they have for their own personal career growth.

## Take Action:

This tactic is all about how to activate a new employee's potential in their first ninety days with you. Wherever you are in your organization, there is something you can do to help new talent get a strong start in your organization. Here are some action steps as examples. Use them as a springboard to imagine more ways to help everyone achieve mastery, plug into the team culture, and improve the transfer of positive culture to everyone on the team.

**If You're on the Frontline:**
- Think about what "mastery" looks like for you in your role. Is there anything in your training that was missed, or processes you could use more familiarity with in order to do your job well or support team members better? Look for ways to solidify your strengths and plug in to processes more effectively to reduce your own burnout and find more satisfaction in your work.

- Identify who on your team you can transfer skills or culture to. If there are opportunities to become a Navigator or peer mentor, take the chance to learn more about leading and developing others. If no formal program exists, find ways in your current routine to keep passing on knowledge and positive connection to team members anyway.

**If You're a Manager or Supervisor:**

- Analyze your system for receiving feedback and assessing the progress of new employees as they go through their first ninety days. Even long-term employees can benefit from progress checks and mastery assessment conversations.

- Use a coaching check-in to ask each of the people you lead where they are feeling confident, where they could use more training or input, and how you are doing on delivering the quality of leadership you promised them. This two-way accountability will help you grow as a leader and elevate your whole team's success.

**If You're an Executive Leader:**

- Evaluate your company's current employee engagement process and identify who could take on the role of S.T.A.Y. Ambassador, becoming the person who ensures the twelve-week onboarding plan is well executed for each new employee. Strategize the kind of training and direction they need to pull each new employee into the S.T.A.Y. Process at your organization.

- Get curious about the kind of training your managers, supervisors, and peer mentors have received which is targeted at improving their communication and people development skills. Being able to do the work itself is not the same as being able to equip and motivate others to do work the way you want it done. Put structures and processes in place to develop these employee's culture and skill transfer skills in a systematic way.

# Activation Tactic #3:
## *Build FUNctional Endurance*

I f "having fun at work" seems like a luxury—something that companies like Google care about, involving ultimate frisbee tournaments and team building at adventure resorts—you're missing out on the kind of powerful fun that humans have when they use their strengths. People are unique individuals who find fulfillment and satisfaction when they use their abilities to accomplish meaningful goals and are recognized by those around them for their efforts.

When I work with leaders, their first assumption about helping people have more fun at work is that they need to offer fun that diverts from work. While I'm all for celebrations, rewards, and culture-building adventures, the shortest distance between a worker and fun is using their strengths to get that work done. Let's think of it as creating FUNctional endurance in our employees. One of the greatest threats to the talent quotient at our organizations is the loss of employees due to burnout. The employee simply says "I can't do this anymore" or "no paycheck is worth this." They lose endurance. Strengths are a powerful way to restore this endurance, and get our existing employees back in top FUNctioning shape.

Many of us have gotten so used to management by paycheck that we think getting our employees to work is about creating the right pressure through goals, accountability, and oversight. We would be shocked by what happens if we shift the engagement dynamic and set our teams up to work inside their strengths to accomplish their goals.

The top skill our people need in order to lead others is self-awareness. If you put a hundred excellent leaders into a room, they will have a broad mix of strengths, preferences, and personality styles. What makes them great leaders is that they understand themselves well enough to bridge beyond their own natural tendencies and connect and invest in others.

Personality and strengths are a great place for your employees and your leadership team alike to begin deepening their understanding of themselves and others. But remember, personality and strengths profiles are tools; don't use them as weapons. As your leaders learn their own strengths and weaknesses, set the expectation that the understanding becomes a tool for lifting and activating their teams, not stereotyping and condescending to others with different gifts.

At the end of the day, the resilient, high-performing, dynamic team is one where everyone learns from one another's strengths. When we do this we both honor the natural affinity people have for things and support their leadership in areas of strength, and we also encourage personal growth by following the example of those who are naturally strong where we are not.


## Macro Level Strengths: Put People in the Right Roles

We'll talk in a minute about how any person can use their strengths to increase their endurance and excellence in executing any job they find themselves in. Using micro-level adjustments to shift into one's strengths to do something is a powerful skill we can all use every day. But there's also a macro-level perspective we want to apply to strengths first.

When you're hiring an employee, experience counts for a lot. So does education and learned skills. But when we put someone into a position that requires them to behave in contrast to their natural personality or core gifting, they are fighting a tougher battle. When we evaluate applicants and begin working with employees we can ensure a better fit by recognizing the personality types and natural giftings that harmonize with that role.

If the charge nurse you need for a rural clinic will need high cultural sensitivity and advanced connection skills you cannot simply pick the most clinically-qualified candidate from the stack of résumés. Someone with a natural people orientation will have more functional endurance in that role.

If you're trying to activate a new employee's talent and recognize they are having to work against the grain of their natural gifts to do it, it's worth evaluating how a big-picture change might be necessary to move this employee in the direction of their gifting.

There are many strengths and personality tests out there. One I use extensively to help teams position their talent well is the DISC Personality Strengths. If you assess yourself and your team for DISC personality, it will measure the levels of your motivational strengths out of four possibilities: Driven, Inspiring, Supportive, Conscientious. While different coaches and consultants adjust the labels—some using "dominant" or "cautious" for the D and C of DISC—the traits that are measured are stable regardless of which term is used for the label.

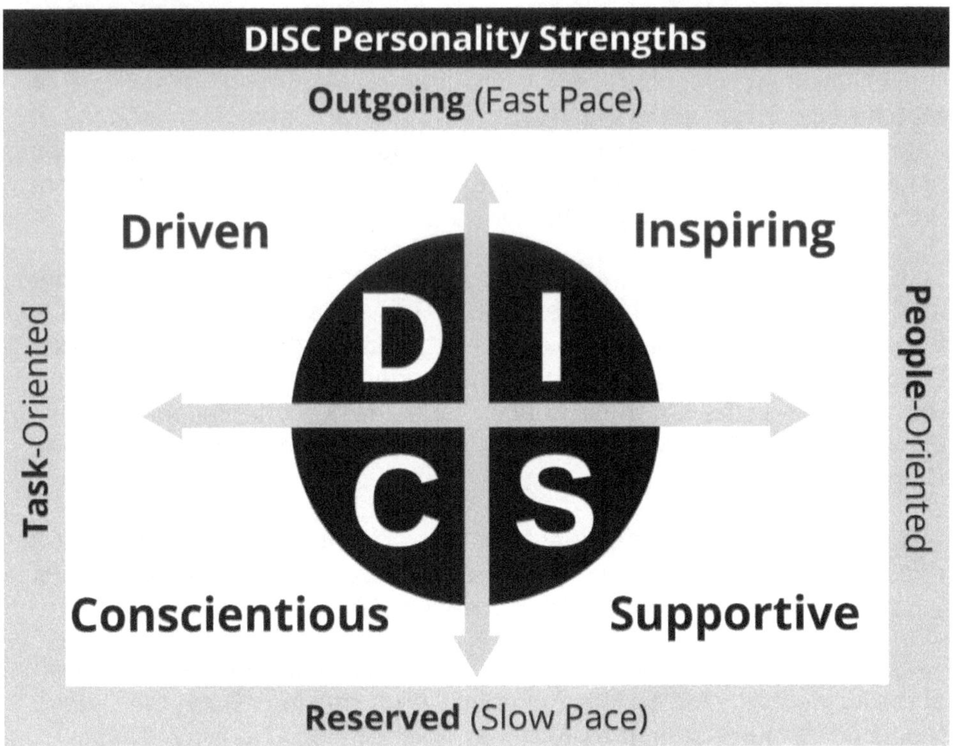

Some companies use a DISC assessment to help them choose between applicants, looking for natural gifting to support the heavy lifting the role requires. Other employers use DISC as part of their S.T.A.Y. development process to improve their ability to communicate with, connect to, and provide authentic motivation for the team member according to their gifting.

This model of strengths can be most useful in a workplace because the simplest version of it consists of just two questions. Their answers give guidance about how to more effectively communicate with, connect to, and support the efforts of the other person.

These two questions are:

Question 1: "Does this person seem **fast paced, or slow paced?**"

Question 2: "Does this person seem **people-oriented, or task-oriented?**"

Learning how to ask and answer these two questions about people drastically increases our social intelligence. Adjusting to support or match the other person's pace instantly increases a sense of connection. Noting someone's task or people orientation guides us on what information they will find more compelling and useful, and what priorities they are serving at the moment.

Combine the two answers and it reveals which of the four dominant strengths that individual is expressing. Someone presenting with slow pace and people orientation is showing the strength of Supportiveness. Do they present a fast pace and people orientation? They are showing the Inspiring trait. Slow pace and task orientation reveals Conscientiousness. While a fast pace and task orientation expresses Drivenness.

Even answering these questions correctly in the moment doesn't necessarily show us what someone's core blend of strengths is. But it's a great starting point for offering connection and support at work.

If you're in a position to test for strengths, doing so can help with activating your employee's potential and making sure they have functional endurance in their role.

Another way to incorporate strengths to activate your employee's potential begins in the first ninety days but extends throughout their entire life at your company. It is part of the Individual Development Plan you co-create with the new employee.

The first portion of onboarding focuses on bringing a new employee through the Universal Training Pathway so they get into the flow of the company culture. But really getting the most out of each employee comes from helping them achieve personal mastery and individualized growth toward their potential.

We talked in the S.T.A.Y. Development Process section about how each employee's Individual Development Plan is designed to help them keep increasing skills and competencies. Sometimes that means promotions or role changes. Use strengths testing to ensure all of the development and progress planned for the employee moves them deeper and deeper into their strengths.

## S.T.A.Y. Development Process

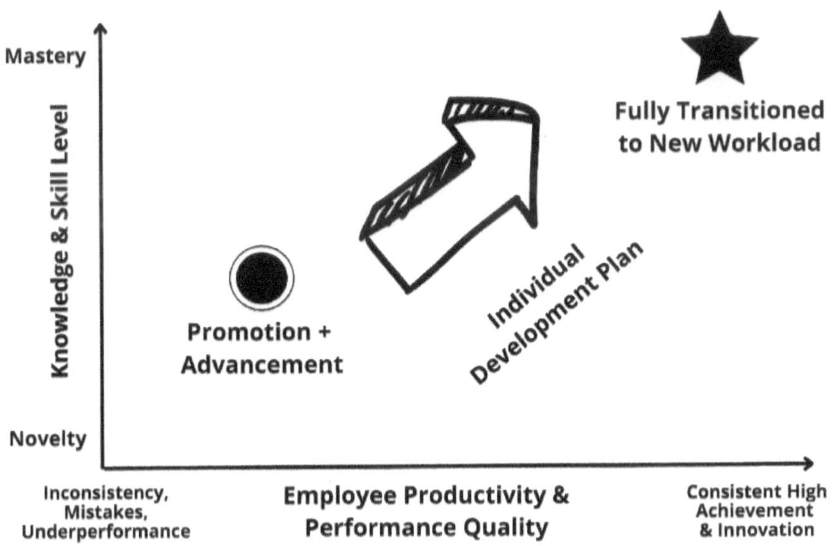

# How To Boost Creativity & Innovation

More often than not, our company's competitive advantage grows in direct proportion to the level of creativity and innovation of our teams. Speed is often a product of inspiration, and employees who are highly engaged move quickly and often make surprising connections that can amplify a company's success.

Stagnation kills. But how often do we spend all of our time as managers trying to get our employees to simply do what is already known? We do this because a management mindset aims for a predictable result. But most of our companies won't even be around in five years if we don't find ways to work faster, better, or in different directions to meet the needs of our stakeholders with innovation and creativity.

Costs are rising, uncertainty is rampant. We can't play it safe trying to get the same old predictable results. But there is great risk in trying new things. Some of them won't work out. So how do we foster the kind of innovation that will ignite our success rather than burning our reserves? We activate the strengths and gifting of each employee on the team.

When an employee is working from their strengths, the insights and ideas they bring to the team are of a higher caliber. They also tend to arrive with a level of energy that will be needed if that idea is put into action.

If a team has follow-through problems, strategic implementation deficiencies, or consistency issues, it's often because they aren't working from their strengths. "Fake it 'til you make it" breaks down in the daily grind. Sustainable success comes from authentic strengths.

## Dirty, Boring Jobs

Sometimes when people talk about working from their strengths, they paint a picture so rosy it feels like a fantasy. "Sure" we say, "getting up and doing only the things you're best at, the things you can do with ease and excitement would be nice. But I don't have that luxury. Stuff has to get done!"

Unpleasant, time-consuming, or repetitive work is a fact of life. But using your strengths is not only possible when doing "fun" tasks. Using your strengths is a way to put fun, satisfaction, and energy into whatever kind of task you're doing. Working from your strengths doesn't mean avoiding unpleasant, repetitive, or boring tasks. Instead, using strengths to do these tasks reduces the toll they take on us.

The leader who says "email is not my strength" is making excuses. The employee who says "I'm just a late person" isn't really talking about their strengths and weaknesses. Whether you use StrengthsFinder, VIA Strengths, or DISC Assessment to discover your strengths, you can use whatever your strengths are to meet the demands of your workload.

Sometimes it takes mental flexibility on the part of the leader to allow new ways of doing work to become part of accepted practice. But think of it this way, instead of staying attached to everyone doing things the way that "everyone does them," what if you stayed attached to the true goal, and challenged your team to find ways to use their strengths to get there in a reliable and accountable way?

## The Quick Fix: Micro-level Strengths

I'm not much of a quick fix guy, because I know solving the root problem is always going to be better than a Band-Aid. But there is one quick and simple approach to getting people into their strengths, and it doesn't even require changing people's workload or role.

Sometimes when I talk to people about getting everyone on the team into their strengths so they can thrive at work, the pushback I receive says "there are some things that just need to be done and no one wants to do them."

Maybe it's a repetitive or unpleasant task. Maybe it's dealing with an inherently frustrating situation. Maybe it's a task that everyone hopes to outgrow—and no one sees as a "passion project." That's okay.

Strengths and personality gifts are not the icing on your work cake— nice to have, but ultimately a luxury. Strengths are the highest gear your life engine is capable of running in. It's the heavy lifting capacity each human has. Switching into strengths doesn't mean doing pleasant or easy work. Switching into strengths means doing whatever work is at hand in a way that affirms and draws on your true power.

And like using any muscle, working from your strengths increases the energy and power you have to work again tomorrow. Like a good workout, you still need rest and a healthy meal, but if you keep fueling the muscle, that muscle gets stronger and more flexible with intelligent use.

You can (and probably should) take a quality personality or strengths assessment to learn more about how to live in that strong gear. But sometimes we need something faster, and easier to use with people we don't know very well. Some days we need an easy way to shift from doing work in a draining way to doing it in an energizing way.

When it comes to strengths, here's an easy way to do that. Switch your driving orientation.

In the DISC Personality Assessment, the researchers use the terms "people oriented" and "task oriented" to divide our strengths into two categories. Many of us can be people oriented at some times and task oriented at others, while others of us live full time in one orientation or the other.

It doesn't matter if you're a switcher or in one mode full time, if you're feeling drained—or see that the person you're working with is drained—ask yourself "am I focused on people, or tasks and information right now?"

A people orientation could be thinking in terms of meeting someone's need, modeling "how someone else did this" or even using social energy to get a task done by co-working or asking for input. We often switch to people orientation by thinking of a person or group and seeking to connect with or serve them, or by being inspired or energized by the stories or feedback of others.

A task or information orientation tends to look like a preoccupation with data, tracking progress, focusing on accomplishing tasks or projects, or visualizing achievement in an objective way. Task orientation is energized by getting to **done**, or visualizing the impact or meaning of what is being accomplished.

Both gears work. If you are feeling drained, try switching. Help your employees to experiment with switching to see if it re-energizes them.

If the work has become all about the data, the accomplishment, being right, or making progress on tasks, stop and look for the people. Look for a person to partner with or to get feedback from. Look for who benefits from or needs the work you're doing to move forward. Look for the human meaning.

If the work is overrun with people, too many voices to please, or time eaten up with meetings and updates, can you pause the interaction and look just at the work, the numbers, or the question you are trying to answer? Do you need to stop all the conversations and create a simple visual tracker to see where you're at on a project, and carve out progress data points to reclaim your energy?

Learn how to do this for colleagues and employees and you will short circuit burnout and unstick performance blocks. To do this, the leader has to raise the lid on their own self-awareness and be willing to try different ways of leading and communicating. This may require some additional training, study, or even hiring a coach to help create a new level of emotional intelligence. Begin with you, then others.


## People Are a Blend

People are a mix of strengths. It's highly common for someone to have two very different, primary personality strengths. You can imagine how different someone who is Driven (the fast-paced, task oriented person) is from someone who is Supportive (the slow-paced, people oriented person.) But what happens when someone is both Driven and Supportive? It usually means they use their strengths at different times, and the way they use one strength may be altered by the other strengths they have.

People also learn to mask their strengths when they aren't appreciated, and to try to perform as if they hold the strengths that are honored in the workplace. If someone with a high strength of Conscientiousness is working in a workplace where toxic positivity is the way to get ahead, they may silence their critical thinking and risk-avoidance insights in order to avoid "sounding negative." But when things go wrong, the team suffers for having missed out on the critical analysis this person's conscientious side was programmed to offer.

Most workplaces idolize some strengths and demonize others. It's not just the conscientious types who are vilified in some workplaces. I've been to places where the inspiring energy and supportive care were belittled as shallow and naive. In those workplaces, leaders eat their young and the churn of turnover is driven by over-prioritization of achievement or perfection.

Even when you're in an industry that leans heavily toward some strengths, to have a fully functional and agile team, you need all strengths represented and respected.

## Reclaim Fun in the Workplace

Fun for me is work. Don't write me off yet if that sounds terrible to you. I'm like everyone else. When I am connected to my purpose or working in my authentic strengths, I experience fun. If you're a leader who wants high performance from your team, it is in your interest to understand how using strengths makes work fun.

If your people are having fun doing their work, their effectiveness rises and their burnout decreases. Don't expect "fun" to look the same for everyone. For the detail-oriented person, discovering an error or working with mind-bending data can be exhilarating. Whatever task needs to be done, using a natural strength to approach the work will reduce friction, increase the potential for excellence, and reduce the energy drain of working.

## Fun According to Strengths

| What Fun Might Look Like | Barriers to FUNctional Endurance |
| --- | --- |
| **Drivenness** | |
| Making choices<br>Cross things off the list<br>Getting started before others<br>Being set loose on a big goal<br>Taking responsibility to decide<br>Minimizing red tape to get results<br>Overcoming impossible challenges<br>Big goals & large scale projects to own | Perfectionism<br>Lost autonomy<br>No way to win<br>Pointless delays<br>Micromanagement<br>Results not measured<br>Lack of meaningful challenge |

| What Fun Might Look Like | Barriers to FUNctional Endurance |
| --- | --- |
| **Inspiration** | |
| Access to leaders<br>High energy culture<br>Variety or change in work<br>Getting to know coworkers<br>Flexibility & creative freedom<br>Public recognition for excellence<br>Engaging/beautiful environment<br>Team-based interaction and feedback<br>Seeing the impact and reach of the job | Harsh criticism<br>Lack of variety<br>Feeling invisible<br>Depersonalization<br>Unchanging routine<br>Pervasive negativity<br>Overly rigid processes<br>New ideas not welcomed |
| **Supportiveness** | |
| Collaboration<br>Being asked to help<br>Easing pain or suffering<br>Shared goals & scoreboard<br>Receiving gratitude privately<br>Clearly communicated needs<br>Adequate time to gain consensus<br>Showing connection and empathy | Feeling isolated<br>Office politics & cliques<br>No time to listen to others<br>Unfair treatment of anyone<br>Constant change of priority<br>No person behind the project<br>Being forced into the spotlight |
| **Conscientiousness** | |
| Nuanced thinking<br>Time to attend to details<br>Being allowed to prepare<br>Quality problems to solve<br>Opportunity to gain expertise<br>Clear parameters for accuracy<br>Opportunities for critical analysis<br>Having questions answered fully<br>Adequate time to do something well | Being rushed<br>Rapid change<br>No clear process<br>Not being listened to<br>Unqualified leadership<br>Inconsistent standards<br>Being second guessed<br>Inadequate quality information |

Every person is driven and fulfilled by their work according to the nature of their strengths. Imagine for a second how strengths showed up at NASA during the launch, rescue, and return of the Apollo 13 crew. The drivenness of the director to get things done, make impossible decisions with little time, and achieve the prime directive at each stage was crucial. To be successful, the director leaned hard on the precise information, risk assessment, and strategic analysis of the conscientious engineers solving problems on earth and in the spacecraft. Supportive staff bridged the gap to bring various expertise together, advancing the voices that might have been missed and offering tenacious engagement to help everyone pull as a team until everyone was safe. And the possibility-focused inspiring types not only held belief in accomplishing the impossible to begin with, but also kept hope fresh by shifting gears quickly to try new ideas on for size when the original plan failed in multiple ways.

Maybe your workplace will never hold human lives in your hands. Or maybe you're a healthcare organization where more lives are vulnerable this afternoon than have been at risk in all of NASA's decades combined. If you are going to achieve greatness, survive the wilds of the marketplace, and get stronger as the years go by, get your employees to work from their strengths.

## Take Action:

This tactic is all about how using our strengths to do even difficult or unpleasant tasks helps us thrive at work. Wherever you are in your organization, there is something you can do to use your strengths and encourage others to use theirs. Here are some action steps as examples. Use them as a springboard to imagine more ways to shift into the strengths zone.

**If You're on the Frontline:**
- Take a strengths test and experiment with using your natural strengths to do more of the heavy lifting at work. Picking even one strength a week to try to use more can increase energy and reduce burnout.

- Pick three peers and notice at least one thing they seem naturally gifted in. Watch how they do the thing, or ask if they will share their mental process as they approach it. Look for one thing you could try based on their example that might improve your experience with that task or activity.

**If You're a Manager or Supervisor:**

- Get honest about the stereotypes you've put on people, and exchange those limiting labels for true insight on their strengths. Is the "shy" executive who doesn't speak up in morning meetings a reflective thinker? Is the chatty unit assistant relationally gifted? Get to know your people beyond their labels so you can call on their strengths at work.

- Look at team members who are struggling, mistake prone, or behind. Be a real leader and get them into their strengths. Like lifting a heavy load with your legs, if you can get them into their strengths to complete the necessary work, their performance will improve.

**If You're an Executive Leader:**

- At a macro level, placing people in roles where their natural gifts shine is crucial. Increase internal mobility to shift talent in the direction of strengths. Use strengths testing to inform promotions or role changes. Look for ways that failing employees might be equipped and empowered by a shift toward their strengths zone.

- How balanced are the strengths within your organization? Does "the way we work here" make space for people with different gifts to plug into the workplace and elevate the team's performance? Or can only one kind of worker survive the strain of your imbalanced environment?

## Extended Resources

For strengths testing or support developing all the intelligence quotients you need to thrive, visit **HarbourResources.com**. Keep growing your self-awareness and connection skills to unlock your top, sustainable performance.

# Activation Tactic #4:
## *Commit to C² Rounding*

Most leaders do more harm than good when they engage in the practice known in healthcare as "rounding." I've seen it outside medical settings too. The supervisor or big leader swoops in for a drive-by update session. Maybe they toss out a "hi, how are you?" before they lob random information at people or fire off questions from their list of open loops.

Simply showing up may be better than never showing your face to your team. But you can do better. This tactic is called $C^2$ Rounding, meaning the rounding is made up of two Cs that amplify one another: connection and communication. This creates Connecting Conversations.

The primary objective for rounding must be to develop authentic connection to the people you are working with. Connection doesn't just happen. In this tactic we will look at how you can develop connectedness with your team, even if the culture feels hostile and siloed right now. But in order for the round to give a high return on time invested (ROTI), you also need quality communication to take place inside of that connection.

Rounding has come to represent a sort of leadership busywork—checking the boxes that some C-Suite officials decided would make our companies run better. But if you elevate your rounding process to practice Connecting Conversations, you form a pathway for continuous improvement.

If you're new to rounding, think of it as a critical leadership practice that allows managers to connect with their staff and address any issues that may be affecting service, work, or employee morale. By intentionally making the rounds to all employees on a regular basis, managers can hear firsthand what's going well and what issues need to be addressed with or for each employee.

As a relationship development process, rounding helps identify areas for continued training, recognizing successes, and addressing teamwork concerns before they become bigger problems. Without a consistent pathway for two-way feedback of this kind, knowledge and insight gets trapped in your organization. Innovative solutions and high performance stall because insights aren't reaching the people who need to act on them.

One of the reasons poor quality rounding is so detrimental is because employees know the hit-and-miss visits by managers aren't aimed at hearing real feedback. Employees know when the expected answer is "everything's fine."

Appearing to "need help," particularly if they are being asked in front of their peers, can feel like an opportunity to be seen as a low performer. The real culture killers may never be shared with you in a drive-by rounding session. You'll find out when it is too late to fix or you have a major turnover challenge on the team. Many leaders at this point blame the team, saying "I did my rounding and no one ever shared any of these problems with me." But a failed response isn't always the fault of the respondent. If you don't make it safe and positive for your employees to give negative feedback during rounds, that's a failure to lead them well.

Understand this as well, some employees are intimidated by titles. It has nothing to do with you, but rather, who they are. We need to make it safe for them to trust us, or we will continue to get the quick "all is well" so they can hurry the "boss" out of the area.

If you want to attract, activate, and keep talent in your organization, commit to a schedule of Connecting Conversations, maybe even letting your team know rounding has gotten an upgrade. In addition to providing a group "check-in," pull an employee or two aside for Connecting Conversations to create opportunities for deeper insight and building the relationship.

The questions you ask should aim to build connection with the employee, build trust, and seek out any challenges they may be having within the team or scope of work being required in their role.

This is a listening and learning rounding session, not a blame and shame. You might consider using the QLT $C^2$ template as a place to start. To ensure that $C^2$ Rounding is an effective practice, there are some key tips that leaders should keep in mind.

## Connect Consistently

Make this kind of connection rounding a regular part of your routine. The first few rounds need to set the tone and create the positive space for increased connection in response. It will take some consistency before your team will open up. Consistency reduces the surprise and uncertainty that surrounds inconsistent rounding practices. Team members are likely to wonder "what's wrong?" or "who's in trouble?" if your visits don't have a normal rhythm to them

Many of the problems that need to be solved in your organization are complex. There are many different perspectives on the causes and solutions as well. If no consistent feedback mechanism is in place for continuous improvement, that means "fixing problems" becomes a big project that no one has time for. It's like the farming adage, "shovel it while it's small." Often the first signs something is going wrong will show up as chatter or energy shifts that will be obvious if you are consistently connecting with your staff. You can begin preparing to address problems, and even proactively direct your team, if you hear these issues being signaled.

Wear and tear on your team is reduced when this kind of ongoing feedback and support comes from leadership to the team on the frontlines. Part of the burnout your team experiences from the day-to-day issues that pop up comes from feeling left to deal with them on their own. By connection rounding, you interrupt this driver of burnout with small investments of energy. This takes less of your time and makes more of an impact on talent retention than what is required after people have already burnt out.

Why do we talk about this process as a crucial tactic for activating a new employee's talent during onboarding? Because at the start of any employee's work with you, their expectations for feedback, support, and continuous improvement are established. Think of it like you are helping a new employee set their metabolism for long-term growth and resilience by starting off with connection rounding.

Employees who come to believe their leaders don't really want feedback start to tune out warning bells and solutions. What gets rewarded gets repeated. If you reward their input and listen to them when they're new, they will establish a pattern of investing more and more of their best gifts into the team.

Connecting consistently doesn't just mean scheduling regular rounds. It also means showing up with consistent expectations and attentiveness.

Don't give anxious pressure to achieve sometimes, and then ask them to share their deepest secrets the next. Display trustworthy, consistent energy toward your staff so they don't wonder which version of you will walk through the door next. For most leaders, this means taking even three minutes to take a deep breath, shift gears to prepare for listening, and prime your brain with the kind of questions you mean to ask before heading to meet up with the team.

If rounding is about connecting, it stops being about you. Conquer your frenetic energy and unresolved workload, or give it a time out, when you head for rounds. Allow it to be a time when you break away from your urgent tasks to receive feedback and learn from team who follows you.

## Listen Differently

I'm not sure what comes to mind for you when you read the words "active listening." Not all of us, even when we're put in leadership positions, are given training on how to listen in an active way.. To be effective at Connecting Conversations you need to listen differently.

### 1. Set Your Pace for Connection

The first step for making your communication more effective has nothing to do with your words; it's all about the pace you're moving at. Have you ever noticed how high-energy people communicate quickly, while others are more reflective and exhibit slower movements and verbal pace? Someone's "gear" less to do with their intelligence and more to do with their personality strengths. Match the pace of whoever you're communicating with in order to make space for actual connection.

If you're a fast-paced person, slowing down will feel weird and inauthentic at first, but push through those feelings. Use breathing and intentional pauses, so that your counterpart finds it easy to connect with you.

If you're a naturally slow-paced person, preparing to speak and listen faster may take more strategy and preparation. Gather your thoughts ahead of time. Make sure you're hydrated and energetic. You can even use focusing strategies to direct the rounding session at a set of questions so that you're ready to move quickly.

## 2.  Give Active Constructive Responses

The Active Constructive Response (ACR) builds connectedness unlike anything else I've seen. Imagine for a second you're rounding on your tech team during a big system update. You expect to hear about roadblocks and give accountability for milestones. But as soon as you arrive one of the team members hits you with information: "Hey boss we're ten percent ahead of schedule!"

What do you do?

An active response invites the person to build on the good news or elaborate on the information. A constructive response gives positive feedback or encouragement to. Seems like a win-win.

ACR to the team being ten percent ahead of schedule could look like:

- "Wow, how have you all managed that?"
- "Tell me all about it!"

But most of us fall short of this kind of response. We may give a passive constructive response like "great work!"

But what happens after that? The connection falls flat. Instead of taking a win and building on it, you've offered a dead end. It's what I call low-quality praise. It sounds positive, but it does nothing to deepen and activate more of the engagement and potential of the person you're praising.

What's great is, ACR can be used with bad news too. Even negative information offers an opportunity to connect and converse with your team members. And when things are going wrong, rounding can be the pathway to get things back on track.

Imagine instead you're rounding with your healthcare team, and someone says "three of our CNAs quit today." That's information. An Active Constructive Response like "what has that been like?" or "tell me more about what is going on" gives them a chance to share their perspective and deepen your insights.

The one thing we don't communicate enough in these situations is "tell me more." We feel pressed for time, and don't want to encourage complaining, right? Unfortunately, without connecting and communicating with our teams about the positive **and** negative things happening, we never create the sense of trust and connection that's necessary for helping our teams thrive. That connection is the only basis for consistent accountability and being able to push our teams to achieve their best.


## 3. Notice Progress

Rounds should be an opportunity for praise and recognition. Every. Single. Time. There are dozens of ways to unearth achievements and progress to praise. For example, invite all team members to catch one another doing something right (offering a "good catch" mention during rounds rewards the one who did well and the team member who noticed it). You should also acquaint yourself with the learning and productivity goals each team member has so that you can look for evidence of progress or achievement. This can be as simple as saying "Kelly has been working on her proficiency with our new accounting system, and this week she handled all her reports solo for the first time. Way to go developing your mastery, Kelly!"

Sometimes the kind of progress you most need to see on your team is toward culture values like increasing teamwork, attention to detail, customer service mindedness, or personal ownership. Make it clear how team members can progress, and reward their efforts with praise in a group huddle or one on one.

## 4. Give Two-Way Accountability

If you're the leader, you probably already know you need to hold your people accountable. But you've made promises to your team as well. Especially during this onboarding process, you've made promises to new employees about the work they'll do, the support they'll receive, and the way you'll lead them. Rounds are a place for you to check in on how well you're delivering on your promises as a leader.

Give your team permission to give you feedback on your communication, availability, and responsiveness. Offer a mixture of closed-ended questions that make it safer for people to answer, and open-ended questions that open things up for the input you don't know you need. This could look like a closed-ended question about the emails you send, such as, "Do you find the check-in emails I send with updates on the other departments' timelines helpful? If yes, what's useful? If no, where does it break down?" Because this is closed and focused, your team has permission to say "that email is not useful to me because..."

Open-ended questions are still focused, but less structured. Something like "where are we experiencing friction in our productivity?" or "what could keep us from meeting our goals right now?" Open-ended questions about customer experience, employee satisfaction, and productivity bottlenecks can save you time as a leader if your team trusts you to receive their input.

## 5. Follow Through

At the end of the day, you've got to do something with what you learn in rounding, or the connection will dry up. If an issue is identified during rounding, follow up with the employee in a timely manner to address it. Some of our employees have a high value of getting their questions answered; others need you to take action on their behalf. Don't say you want to help if you aren't going to match action to the words.

We're not judged by our intentions, but by our actions. This can feel overwhelming. I've watched leaders abbreviate and put off rounding conversations when they're afraid they can't fix the problems they're certain their employees are going to voice. But hiding away until annual review time is no way to keep talent at your organization.

Connection rounding done frequently is often easier to follow through on than the once-in-a-blue-moon check in made by an overworked manager. Frequent rounds mean enough time for tweaking and small actions to keep problems on the workbench from one round to the next.

One of the ways to follow through on rounding is to solicit feedback from employees on how rounding could be improved and adjust your approach accordingly. As busy as you are, don't forget to get feedback on the timing of your rounds. Is it conducive to the people you need to connect with? If adjustments are needed, make that feedback welcome.

## 6.  Go Deeper with Intentional Questions

Some of the Connecting Conversations you have with your team can be in a group setting. Others are better suited to the quarterly or monthly one on ones you have to support your new and old employees alike individually. Here is a list of questions I share with my clients to show them the kind of intentional, connecting questions that can help us see, understand, and activate the talent on our team well.

- How is your family doing?

- What are the biggest challenges at home right now?

- When things are really good at work what is it about you or the team that seems to make the difference?

- When we're at our best what are we doing differently than when things aren't going well?

- Which team members have you noticed doing a great job that you feel should be recognized for their effort?

- How/what is your leader doing to create a safe work environment and collaboration with the team?

- Are there any issues you have or have not brought to leadership's attention that we need to address?

- What big personal goals or family events are coming up for you in the next three months that we should know about and how can we support you?

- If you weren't being seen as tooting your own horn, what efforts have you been making lately that you'd like to see recognized or hear feedback about?

- Even if it isn't a big deal, what small irritation or frustrating thing about work would be nice to see fixed or improved?

- What have you noticed that is aggravating to yourself or others on the team?

We earn the permission to ask personal questions by developing are relationship and connecting with those we lead. But part of how we earn that permission is by starting to listen now. Don't be irritated if your early attempts to connect yield thin or evasive answers. Pivot to stay curious about whatever area allows them to share their insight with you. Actively listen to what you've been told, and build a basis for trust that increases the quality of responses you get over time.

Every time a colleague opens up and responds to our attempts to connect, it's an honor. Start building this connectedness in the first weeks the new employee is with you, and never stop.

## Round During Onboarding

Like a lot of the things you do for new employees during the activation stage, rounding is one of the practices that is critical for a good start, but doesn't end when onboarding is complete. The way you introduce rounding during an employee's first days sets the tone for the long term.

Make it clear to the employee that while they are getting trained and oriented, your focus on them in rounding will support that. But that as time goes on, rounding, and the feedback process established by it, will continue for the rest of their time with you.

By following these tips, leaders can make $C^2$ rounding an effective tool for improving communication, building relationships, and promoting excellence in employee performance.

Early rounding amplifies the return on investment you will make in that employee's first year as well as the total value they create during their entire time with you. If you miss out on it during their first ninety days, you'll miss out on some of that margin. And it's not just a matter of subtracting the value missed during their first ninety days, you will miss it as a multiplier of their growth and productivity compounding every week and year after.

Getting ongoing feedback on your new employee's experience can help you correct misconceptions, challenge bad habits before they take root, and learn from the fresh perspective of the new hire. Sometimes those new eyes can show you flaws, challenges, and even sinister issues at work in the culture that you can't see. But as this newness wears off, the employee may come to assume you don't care to hear about it.

Problems in a culture don't go away. The seeds of discontent and future turnover are often planted in the first ninety days where the onboarding employee had an issue that none of their leaders cared to hear about or address. Fix these and you slow the talent drain in the future.

## Activate People's Knowledge & Insight

Have you ever noticed that when someone asks you why you did something, you feel a little attacked? Or how when someone shares a tricky problem and asks how you think you'd handle it, you generally have some good advice to offer? This is because the right kinds of questions access our deep insight and instinctive wisdom. The wrong kinds of questions trigger defensiveness.

Questions that start with "why" inherently make people feel defensive. It doesn't matter what your intent is, or how savvy a communicator you are, a "why" question doesn't unlock people's answers. Cut "why" out of your rounding vocabulary. Especially when you need to uncover causes and reasons, use questions that start with "what" and "how" to create the mental access your team needs to their insights.

"What" asks for information. "How" seeks understanding of the process. Asking "what happens when we use this process?" will produce more useful information than "why does the process seem to not work?" "How are we handling this process now?" will give more insight on what's functioning and failing than "why don't we do it the way we've been told to do it?"

Context is also key to helping people be ready for accountability, problem solving, and providing quality feedback you need as a leader. Setting context while rounding is important. Let your visit to the team be more than a pointless fly by. Are you asking for status updates? Are people encouraged to share roadblocks or problems they could use help solving? Are you there to notice progress and give praise for the efforts you have been seeing?

This is why we call this $C^2$ Rounding. It's connection and communication being created by consistent, intentional interaction with your team. We need this to deal with problems and keep our team's talent activated.

Without connection there is no communication, only static and dead air. Remember the old mobile phone commercial? "Can you hear me now?" Without the connection they couldn't talk. Without you connecting to your employees there is no trust, and no ability for you to hear what you need to hear from your team.

## Rounding for Virtual Teams

Maybe you think I use the concept of rounding because I often work with traditional workforces. Maybe you think my background in healthcare team development means this tactic is designed for the healthcare leaders reading this book.

But, rounding is for everyone.

In fact, the lack of a traditional workspace or location-based proximity means that finding a systematic way to do rounds is more important than ever. Whether your company employs a multi-site workforce, hybrid team, or is fully virtual, rounding will help you stay connected to the productivity and momentum of your team members.

How do problems reach your ears before costing excess time, money, or reputation? How do you become aware of barriers, or discover opportunities for growth if you're not keeping your finger on the pulse of the team's daily work?

Project management tools, ticket systems, and performance metrics can bring potential areas for concern or celebration to your awareness. But they do nothing to replace one-on-one, face-to-face connection with each of your employees. If meeting in person is impossible or infrequent, virtual face-to-face time needs to take the place of these rounds. Seeing and focusing on the verbal and non-verbal communication of your employees is key. For employees with disabilities or communication impairments, put in the effort to find a way to connect with them genuinely. The point is to make it possible for them to consistently, and with some ease, communicate with you about what their experience of their work, performance, and the culture is.

# Take Action:

This tactic is all about forming constructive two way connections through Connection Rounding. Wherever you are in your organization, there is something you can do to improve the quality of information flow, and continuous improvement in the work environment, and the productive capacity of the team. Here are some action steps as examples. Use them as a springboard to imagine more ways to help voices be heard and people feel connected in an ongoing way.

**If You're on the Frontline:**
- If your leaders round now, do what you can to match their pace when they stop in. Prepare to speed up or slow down to connect with them better.

- Make the most of opportunities to share your insights, and praise the achievements and progress of others. Doing this will reduce your burnout and improve the positive culture for your coworkers.

**If You're a Manager or Supervisor:**
- Learn how to increase the quality of information you receive in rounds by using Active Constructive Response (ACR). Instead of jumping straight to fixes and correcting others, seek to learn more and understand the perspective being shared.

- Start using better questions to build connectedness with those you supervise. Ask some brave questions about how you're following through on what you've promised, and you'll rise above most leaders your team has ever had.

**If You're an Executive Leader:**

- Assess what form of virtual or in-person rounds would help turn your organization into a learning organization. Continuous improvement grows from effective flow of information, experimentation, and feedback. What large-scale changes need to happen to embed this in your organization?

- Get consistent and intentional with your rounding practice. Round with managers directly beneath you to support their effectiveness and learn continuously yourself. Try "skip rounding" where you bypass the team you manage and talk to their direct reports to learn from deeper in the organization.

# Activation Tactic # 5:
## *Guide & Course Correct*

Mentoring and developing the talent in your organization is one of the most lucrative activities you will undertake. This is because, as Laurie Bassi and Daniel McMurrer put it, "For many companies, employees are the only source of long-term competitive advantage."[46] When researchers talk about measuring the return on Human Capital Management (HCM), they're talking about the impact these mentoring and talent development activities have on the bottom line today and the profit outlook for the future.

Businesses go under every day because of lost battles with cash flow that spring from poorly performing teams. Turnover brings the cost of training, resourcing, and workload maneuvering. During the transition, many companies see dips in customer satisfaction, retention, and recruitment. Innovation takes a back seat to survival. The net result year after year is that your company doesn't reach its potential and profit margins fail to widen.

Like living month to month on a tight paycheck, your company's competitive advantage is vulnerable to mistakes, missed opportunities, and sub-par performance. Instead of stabilizing and expanding existing successes, your team keeps going into the ring to fight for a dwindling pool of half-satisfied customers.

Stabilized workflow, consistent performance, and innovation toward growth don't happen in an annual seminar. The kind of fine tuning that unlocks the potential and excellence of your team happens in the trenches of daily work.

Bringing in coaches and consultants can offer new strategies and experienced help as your team grows. But at some point, all the outside experts in the world can't substitute for one-on-one mentoring and feedback that should be happening for each member of the team from within your organization.

I haven't yet met a manager or leader who had extra time. That means no one has extra time to throw at mentoring to "see if it helps." Leaders need to know exactly where to start and what to do to develop the value and unlock top performance in their people. So, let's talk about what you need to be doing in these mentoring and development interactions. I promise this isn't a section full of spoon-feeding or hand-holding. Let's talk about Human Capital Drivers.

## Human Capital Drivers & Mentoring Goals

Useful research has been done to identify Twenty-Three Human Capital Management (HCM) Practices that fall in five broad categories. Researchers call these the five categories of human capital management drivers. They are Leadership Practices, Employee Engagement, Knowledge Accessibility, Workforce Optimization, and Learning Capacity.[47]

### Human Capital Drivers

| HCM Practices Categories | Human Capital Drivers |
| --- | --- |
| Leadership Practices | Communication<br>Inclusiveness<br>Supervisory skills<br>Executive skills<br>Systems leadership |
| Employee Engagement | Job design<br>Commitment<br>Time<br>Systems |
| Knowledge Accessibility | Availability<br>Collaboration<br>Information sharing<br>Systems |

| Workforce Optimization | Processes<br>Conditions<br>Accountability<br>Hiring<br>Systems |
| --- | --- |
| Learning Capacity | Innovation<br>Training<br>Development<br>Value and Support<br>Systems |

## Make Mentoring Measurable

I'm not big on fancy terms and hard-to-explain, academic mumbo jumbo. So let's call this what it is: a way to make mentoring measurable. Frameworks like this one make it possible to rate where your people are at, and how they're performing in terms of behaviors that really move the needle on your company's long-term growth and profitability.

Teams that use a clear framework, such as this one, can assess the HCM Maturity Score by rating each practice on a scale of one to five with one being low maturity and five being high maturity. Let's take the Human Capital Management Driver called "Leadership Practices." There are specific practices that support your people in having improved maturity in their leadership practices. These include Communication, Inclusiveness, Supervisory Skills, Executive Skills, and Systems Leadership.

Savvy leaders are often skeptical of kitchen-sink coaching; not all time and money spent "encouraging your employees" converts to improved performance at work. So, as you begin working to develop the talent on your team, connect your mentoring goals to these HCM Drivers, which real-world testing has revealed directly impact the long term profitability of your team.

## Showing Up Starts Your Gains

If you're tempted to shelve the rest of this section until you feel like things ease up, slow down, or get better, I want to draw your attention to one of the first drivers every savvy leader can nudge into motion immediately: Learning Capacity. In this driver we have the practices of Innovation (showing new ideas are welcome), Training (providing practical support for employees to reach organizational goals), Development (creating a future through formal career development planning), Value and Support (where leaders show that learning is valued), and Systems (using learning management systems to automate aspects of training).

The following strategy for mentoring your team provides positive investment in each of those practices all in one fell swoop. The longer you engage in developing and mentoring your team, the more gains are amplified exponentially, but you don't have to wait years for this effort to pay off. The talent development process can start today, and your gains will begin accruing.

## Focus your mentoring through four lenses:

1. **The Person** (personality, individuality, strengths)

2. **The Present** (assessing skills, challenges, opportunities, problem-solving)

3. **The Process** (systems, consistency, teamwork, communication)

4. **The Plan** (goals, strategy, personal vision, motivation)

### Engage the Person

Whatever it is your company does, the people you manage are people first. To unlock their talent, you'll need to know more than their résumé and job duties. Start with the Person element, even if you've known, and worked closely with, the person you're mentoring for some time.

Some teams use formal personality assessments to open up a shared language about the individuality and complementary strengths represented by team members. Other leaders will have informal conversations where they work to develop positive communication and connection with the people they manage.

These personality differences range from their favorite coffee order to discovering what form of praise and recognition the employee finds most meaningful. It involves discovering how that employee sees themselves, their role, and how they fit into the team culture.

Finding shared interests or common experience can bring positive energy to the mentoring process. But remember: employees see right through our attempts to manipulate them or put them into boxes that make them easier to manage. Paying attention to them as a person moves the needle in our leadership performance because it helps us listen to and intentionally develop that person.

Questions are a great way to gather a better understanding of the employee as an individual. Questions like: "What motivates you? What are you passionate about outside of work?" Or questions aimed at their individual experience of the workplace: "What do you believe your greatest talents and skills are, and how do you think they should be used in your role?"

When you start with the individual and get a picture of where they want to go, you have been granted a priceless gift as their leader: a window into their intrinsic motivation. When you need to challenge inefficiencies, push for skill strengthening, or foster teamwork and innovation, you will have something to guide you. Show the employee how the success you're trying to achieve for your organization fits with their individual pursuit of success. If you can do that, you will align the will of the employee with the forward progress of your organization. That's where real growth comes from.

When mentoring and leading across generational divides, honoring and activating each employee as an individual can be the lynchpin to your success. Working with Gen Xers, both subsets of Millennials (Early Gen Y and Generation iY), and the Generation Z who followed them, means an intensification of the drive all of your employees have to be seen as individuals.

Previous generations are characterized by accepting some of the cultural norms in the workplace. But from "Baby Busters" on to the youngest employee prospects you'll have in the next decade, you are now leading a group born into a world of unprecedented independence, self-expression, and choice. Where previous generations might have pushed to achieve the "right goals" for career advancement, later generations are increasingly driven to discover the "right goals for me."

For this reason, the same incentives, social pressure, and consequence structure for poor performance will not work consistently across the generations you are leading. In fact many of your most effective techniques will backfire if used on the wrong employee. While we can't stereotype employees by decade and manage them by generation, being generationally aware can give us a better starting place for experimentation and discovery when developing the strengths and performance of an employee. Being aware of highly-shared generational values can help us avoid destroying trust, and prevent unnecessary barriers to creating intellectually diverse and skill-dense teams.

## Pause & Apply

Before we move ahead, bring one of your employees to mind. What do you know about this person? What do you need to learn? What is their personality type? Do you have an assessment like DISC, or another tool, to help you understand how they receive and deliver communication? Do you know this person's career goals and how fulfilled they feel?

Every person deserves to be led well by a leader who values them as an individual, not just for what they produce while on the clock. Be the leader you wish you had, for each person on your team.

## Engage the Present

We often start a coaching or mentoring relationship with employees because we have a problem to solve. We can shoot ourselves in the foot if we rush into problem solving without building psychological safety and respect within this relationship. If you successfully engage the person first, improving skills, stabilizing productivity, or solving chronic problems becomes an ongoing process. The longer you engage real-time reflection, praise, and feedback, the more the employee grows in effectiveness and engagement. In order to make a positive change, we need to demonstrate that we have confidence in the value of the employee, and that they have value to bring to the organization. From that place of safety, we need an honest assessment of what the current status is.

That status could be information about the employee's performance, their level of understanding, or how skilled they are in various areas. Some attributes can be measured externally, but sometimes the best assessment comes when the leader helps an employee self-assess.

The present also includes environmental stressors, relational friction, and external demands the employee is facing as they try to do their work. Sometimes the leader is part of the pressure, adding accountability to help the employee focus on growth. But sometimes the employee is experiencing stressors the leader isn't aware of.

You aren't your employee's therapist, and yes, sometimes you'll need to address performance issues in the present that the employee would rather ignore. So here are three words that are every coach's best friend: What, If, and How.

Starting questions with the word "what" is one way to get a clear picture of the present. "What seems like the most difficult goal on your plate right now?" or "What has your experience of onboarding been since you joined us last month?" If you know there's a problem, using "what" can help deepen your understanding, without sounding like an invitation to complain. Try something like "what part of the process seems to break down most often?" or "what happens when you collaborate with that vendor?"

Using **If** is a way to hold onto the objective without causing pressure. It plays nice with **What** and **How** to help your coachee problem solve, without feeling boxed into a corner. It's a formula:

**If + What / How = Insight**

Examples:

**If** we need to get the turnaround time on these projects down to the estimate, **how** could we shave time off the process?

**If** we didn't have to do it the way we've always done it, **what** would you consider trying to speed the process up?

**If** we need to win three new contracts by the end of the quarter, **what** would we need to focus on and **how** can we avoid unnecessary distractions?

**Pause & Apply**

Let's put this into practice right now before going to the next step. Identify a challenge within your team. What seems to be stuck or not working? Bring the team, or a small sampling of the team, together and apply the above formula to the challenge.

## Engage the Process

In the previous section, my examples were filled with processes and systems. It's one thing to solve a single problem that may help us today. Solving an inefficiency in a process though, helps us every day afterward. This is why I talk about the "S.T.A.Y. Process," not just "onboarding." The way many companies do onboarding is simplistic. It's seen as a brief stint newcomers must spend learning what is expected and how it's done in their new role. But the simple actions and responsibilities assigned will never have as much impact on your new employee's performance as the processes they learn and engage.

In fact, processes aren't just how things get done. Processes help us retain people for the long term, allowing their skill and knowledge to stay with the company and increase our company's competitive advantage.

I'm a believer that when something isn't working in our organization we should first evaluate the process or system before we start to place blame on any person. This isn't because I'm a nice guy; it's because most of our results flow from systems and processes.

If you have a process—even a poor process—you've got something that can be systematically improved upon. You've got something that is consistent. If you don't have a process, success seems to happen by magic and failure fills in the gaps between magical moments.

Some work seems to lend itself to processes in an obvious way. But even work that seems highly individualized, situation-specific, or filled with variety, involves processes if you know how to look at them. Anytime we develop a training plan, or map out the flow of work for a new hire's duties, we have the opportunity to identify processes and strengthen them.

Often, employees who resist thinking about their work as having a system or a process do it because they don't want their job to seem like something "anyone can do following this process." That's because most of us have experience working in environments where management saw their employees as completely replaceable. Leaders don't do themselves any favors when they try to adopt management practices designed to make work "any monkey can do." This is perhaps the worst version of what a good process is meant to do.

When you're coaching an employee, identify whether it is an external process you want to help your employee learn, or if the employee is competent enough to have their own unique process that needs troubleshooting. A process can be as simple as asking "what's the first thing you do when you arrive at work?" It can be task specific, such as how to handle a particular piece of information, or apply globally to how they get work done, such as batching like tasks, or operating a ticket system that honors " first in, first out," etc.

## Pause & Apply

Ok, before we move on, let's evaluate a process or system. Let's take an example from one of the many hospitals where I've consulted: client satisfaction scores reflect the patient experience process. From the moment the patient enters the facility until they are discharged, there is a system and workflow impacting their experience. I challenge every leader in this environment to be a "secret shopper." Start in the parking lot and move through each step of the process and look for areas to improve along the way. This can be easier to do for our non-healthcare clients, but even without faking medical needs, you can shadow the progression of whoever your client is through the arrival, engagement, and release processes. When you're shadowing, **do not** start fixing things. Make notes and then invite your team into the change discussion to make the process better.

What processes or systems is your team complaining about but just saying "this is the way we have always done it?" I call that TWWADI disease, as shared with me by my friend Diane Caine. Leaders must cure TWWADI on your teams by evaluating processes and then challenging them to change.

## Engage the Plan

For some of us, "plan" is truly a four letter word. If you're coaching someone who hates planning, you've got a challenge. But even if your coachee values and honors the plan they're supposed to follow, they will face the reality we all do each day: executing our plans is harder than dreaming up solutions.

Even for us "doers," we need the daily, weekly, or monthly retrospective to check our efforts against the plan we made. Is our effort matching up to what we intended? How well does the plan work? Did we even really execute the plan well enough to know whether it's working or not? What blueprint are we using to track progress, focus action, and step out our good intentions?

Vision is awesome, and without it we don't know what we're aiming for in the long run. But we need a plan if we're going to step our way toward that victory each day. A plan takes the bright light of our vision and maps out the mundane, practical, clear steps we must take to take ourselves and our company into that light.

Most of us pay the cost of poor planning every day. Maybe it's your own lack of plan, or you lead employees who arrive at work without any real idea how to attack the day or week. Many of our team members simply punch the clock and go through the motions—rinse and repeat each day, putting out fires but never advancing a clear goal. I'm not saying they aren't working hard, but the work becomes routine and mundane and they aren't acting on a plan to improve things for the team, themselves, or the customer.

To move from good to better to best, we must engage in a plan to get just a little bit better each day. In *Atomic Habits*, James Clear shares the data behind getting a thirty-seven percent return on an annual basis by focusing on a one percent improvement each day.[48] I love numbers like that. A one percent improvement will not sap our strength; but a thirty seven percent improvement drastically changes our success trajectory.

What is your plan to improve in small increments? Sadly many leaders and organizations are reactive and are often trying to make thirty-seven percent returns at the end of a quarter or year, without the one percent improvements required to get there.

I recently completed a major bucket list goal in my life by hiking to the bottom of the Grand Canyon and then back to the top. The descent was over seven miles and over 4700 feet of cumulative elevation loss to the bottom of the canyon. I had to then hike a separate ten mile trail and reclaim that 4700 feet of elevation to return to the top.

When I set this goal almost a year earlier, I had to create a plan to prepare my body and my mind for success. I didn't just show up and do the hike hoping to carry the forty pounds of necessary gear to survive the round trip trek. I spent eight months carrying this same weight on multiple preparation hikes to make sure I was successful. Meaningful victories don't just happen.

## Your Daily GPS

I sometimes talk about planning using the illustration of putting your visionary coordinates into a GPS to map step-by-step guidance for conquering the next piece of road. Instead of a Global Positioning System, think of your plan's GPS as a Goal Pursuing System. My high performance planner and daily action worksheet uses this mindset to think about the day's action plan.

When you're mentoring and guiding your employees to grow, having the right planning tool can be the difference between vague platitudes and useful coaching through a measurable, improvable, concrete, daily or weekly plan. I say daily and weekly, because most of us do quarterly or monthly progress reviews at most, when what's needed are daily and weekly planning workflows.

While it's crucial to have a way to look at what's happened in the past, it's important for your coaching to get into the present. Your coachee doesn't just need a second set of eyes looking at "what happened this quarter." They need a collaborator to help them make choices today that impact this week. If your coaching stays in the past, it can increase anxiety and feel like a drain on time. Remember the connection between planning and deployment; that connection is the present. Even small improvements in your employee's ability to engage the present escalates their success on a daily and weekly basis.

Maybe you played a sport or an instrument growing up. The coach or instructor didn't wait until after the game or concert to teach you, guide you, help you perfect your technique, and make improvements did they? No, they were with you daily, teaching, course correcting, encouraging, and developing you to make new decisions and technique changes before setting you up to succeed.

They also didn't wait until the end of the year to give you a performance review only to surprise you with negative feedback. It would be ludicrous to handle sports or musical training this way. So why do we do this in the workplace? How do we expect people to get better when we only give feedback when someone has made a mistake or at the end of the year? Don't we need the same continuous improvement during the year that any athlete or musician needs to perform well?

In our QLT Culture Framework we recommend consistent coaching as well as a daily team rally to get your team's daily GPS coordinates set. I've had leaders balk at this idea. They say "Mike we just do the same thing day in and day out and nothing really changes. I just want them to come to work and do their job." But friend, if they aren't performing how they need to, something needs to change. A daily GPS rally can inspire new attitudes and behaviors, connect them to purpose, or be an opportunity to celebrate a win for the team.

I say leader, start with you! I have a framework for the attitude and mindset I teach. SOAR and serve.

> **S**tart on Purpose—Why am I here today? What outcomes am I hoping to drive?

> **O**wn your Attitude—Is my attitude one that lifts others up or pulls them down?

> **A**ct like a Leader—Am I taking people to a new place or leaving them where they were yesterday?

> **R**eally, really care about the MVP's—Mission, Values and People—Do I really care about the people I lead, or do I just care about looking good for the people who lead me?

If you, the leader, aren't SOARing, you'll never get your team to soar or serve with purpose.

If you want to quit losing talent, then remember this:

"If it is to be, it is up to me."

## Take Action:

This tactic is all about treating the people at your organization like the appreciable assets they really are. Wherever you are in your organization, there is something you can do to participate in a culture of continual improvement and full engagement. Here are some action steps as examples. Use them as a springboard to imagine more ways to grow as a person, engage the present reality, improve the processes that create success, and plan for an inspiring future.

**If You're on the Frontline:**

- Check in on your own planning process for daily and weekly action. Do you need a **Goal Pursuing System** to map out a motivating future that starts today? Get a free printable resource at **HarbourResources.com.**

- What are your personal processes? Workflows and habits are great places to focus for your one percent, daily improvement. Look for ways to increase speed, accuracy, clarity, or connection with the rest of your team and unlock higher achievement.

**If You're a Manager or Supervisor:**

- Look at the year ahead of you. What is your structure and frequency for getting to know the people on your team and expand their potential? What schedule for coaching and mentoring will maximize their potential and fuel the success you are responsible for?

- Assess the mentoring and coaching skills of the people on your team and see where you can transfer process improvement and planning skills to others so that they can help teammates grow as well.

**If You're an Executive Leader:**

- Assess your own mindset about employees: are they an expense or an asset? Is your organization taking advantage of the greatest potential competitive advantage it has by unlocking the Human Capital Drivers in your employees through mentoring and development?

- How hard is it for process improvements to be made in your organization? Do employees pay for speaking up, or are they rewarded for helping the organization improve? Top leadership has to set the culture up to become a learning organization. Take ownership for this shift in your company and leave a legacy of growth.

# Afterword: Make the Culture Stick

So often as leaders, we're pulled in conflicting directions: dream for the future, or survive today. Dreaming inevitably falls to the level of infrequent luxury, and survival swallows our everyday focus. We can't let this happen.

What keeps us stuck in the competition between the troublesome now and our vision of the future is often our own mindset. We get set on knocking down short-term "wins" and avoiding "losses." Getting real wins is key, but if we're not careful we can lead our teams into chasing metrics that get us nowhere, setting goals that keep us locked into a finite game.

Thinkers like Simon Sinek make a distinction between finite thinking and infinite thinking—asking leaders to recognize the world of difference it makes if you see your work as competing in a finite game or an infinite game. Finite games take place for set periods of time, according to established rules, and leave a clear winner or loser.

But how often is that the kind of game we're in at work? Not only is our work ongoing, the rules of the game aren't clearly established. There isn't only one way to play, score, and fumble. Instead, our lives take place on the field of the infinite game: any number of players can come and go from the field, playing according to a variety of often-changing rules, and there is no ending point where everyone agrees on the winner.[49]

I love what happens when someone stops for a second to refocus on the infinite game in their life and workplace. The rewards of winning a finite game may feel good for a second—"we beat you" kind of victory laps. But the rewards of playing well in an infinite game are meaningful, fulfilling, and have the potential to last well beyond our tenure or even our lifetime.

Even if your company identity is not idealistic, if you don't have a humanitarian charter or benevolent goal, every individual in your organization can come to work with an infinite game mentality and be more successful every day. Frontline workers, middle management, even seasonal and volunteer workforces become engaged and successful when they connect to the lasting achievements of playing their part of the game well.

The first edition of this book took just four tactics and taught them as a basis for creating a talent lock inside your organization. With my team at Harbour Resources, we're excited to expand the playbook to include twenty tactics that support the infinite development and productivity of your workforce. This is the next part of my contribution to the infinite game you are playing in your workplace.

Keeping talent inside your company, regardless of who comes and goes, isn't just a pipe dream. You as the leader can move your organization toward locking the human resources, and insights they develop, into your organization for years to come.

So which tactic is your business ready to profit from? Which strategy will put your company at a significant advantage against your competition? If you're reading this, you're a leader who is working to strengthen your organization. Let us know how you use this, and which strategies you find most valuable in this season of growth.

As the leader in charge of the results, remember: you are the driver of success. Who you are **be**coming will be echoed by the team that follows you, and embodied by the systems and processes carved out by your team each day. **Be**come the leader who creates the culture that attracts, develops, and keeps great talent, and everything else you need to do gets easier.

When we are constantly spinning our wheels replacing people, we never get to focus on the more important objectives of leadership. This book has been your call to quit losing talent by implementing the systems to make it happen. Don't forget the power of pursuing the goals and vision of your organization with practical actions every day. Build out your own GPS—Goal Pursuing System—so that you can make measurable, meaningful progress on a daily, weekly, and monthly basis.

I'm going to be here, cheering you on, challenging your limiting beliefs, and offering ideas when you need something new to try. Don't hesitate to reach out if I can speed you on your journey. The world is screaming for leadership today more than ever. Be the leader who calms the fears, doubts, and voices. This is your time. This is the time to be a leader who quits losing talent!

*Mike Harbour*

# Acknowledgments

I would like to acknowledge the doubts, fears, and voices in my own head that prevented me from sharing my ideas in a book for far too long! Because of these voices, I became a better speaker, teacher and curator of ideas that have helped thousands of people over the years, and I finally got over the fear of putting the ideas in a book.

Special thanks to Morgan Hendrix who has spent countless hours helping me transfer the ideas in my head into a book to help others. She has listened, learned, and leveraged the thousands of ideas and hours of audio and video I have produced to help put this book together in a useful way for the reader. Morgan, you're a rockstar!

Connie Harbour has been a constant encourager, proofreader, and cheerleader, pushing me to keep living the dreams I have to help others grow. She has spent hours attending my speaking and coaching sessions to help capture my ideas and build out the tools that you can use to implement the ideas of this book. Connie, you're every man's dream!

This book wouldn't be possible without the thousands of leaders I've interviewed and served over the last twenty-five years and counting. I have learned from every conversation. Helping companies and innovative leaders use these principles to improve their talent and strengthen their cultures has been a privilege. To each of my clients, past and present, I say, "Thank you!"

Visit **HarbourResources.com** for more free content and specialized
training to equip you and your team to thrive in
today's marketplace.


Call us at 501-503-1149 or
visit our website: www.HarbourResources.com

# Notes


1 Richard Branson. Twitter, March 27, 2014. https://twitter.com/richardbranson/status/449220072176107520.

2 Daniel Kahneman, *Thinking, Fast and Slow* (New York: Farrar, Strauss and Giroux, 2011).

3 Modern Italian speakers will spell this phrase *saper vedere*, and pronounce it differently than my colleagues and I learned when studying the wisdom of Leonardo Divinci.

4 Bill Denison. "Leonardo da Vinci's scientific visualizations: 'Saper verdere' or knowing how to see." *University of Maryland Center for Environmental Science Integration and Application Network,* May 1, 2017. https://ian.umces.edu/blog/leonardo-da-vincis-scientific-visualizations-saper-verdere-or-knowing-how-to-see/.

5 "Wayne Dyer Quotes," BrainyQuote.com, BrainyMedia Inc, last modified 2023, https://www.brainyquote.com/quotes/wayne_dyer_384143.

6 "Number of visitors to the Louvre Museum in Paris, France from 2007 to 2022 (in millions)," Statista, accessed 7/12/22, https://www.statista.com/statistics/247419/yearly-visitors-to-the-louvre-in-paris/.

7 Jim Collins, *Good to Great: Why Some Companies Make the Leap...And Others Don't* (New York: HarperCollins Publishers, 2001).

8 This leader's name was changed to protect her privacy.

9 Viktor Frankl, *The Will to Meaning* (New York: PLUME/Penguin, 2014), 39.

10 John Maxwell, *The 21 Irrefutable Laws of Leadership*, (Nashville: Thomas Nelson, 2007), 39.

11 Gabriella Rosen Kellerman and Martin Seligman, *Tomorrowmind: Thriving at Work with Resilience, Creativity, and Connection—Now and in an Uncertain Future*, (New York: Atria Books, 2023), 80.

12 "Top 12 Employee Retention Strategies." Profit.co. Accessed 9/30/23, https://www.profit.co/blog/employee-engagement/top-12-employee-retention-strategies-that-work/.

13 Lee Colan, "A Lesson from Roy A. Disney on Making Values-based Decisions," *Inc.,* July 24, 2019. https://www.inc.com/lee-colan/a-lesson-from-roy-a-disney-on-making-values-based-decisions.html.

14 "Burnout," Psychology Today, accessed July 8, 2023, https://www.psychologytoday.com/us/basics/burnout.

15 Peter M. Senge, *The Fifth Discipline: The Art and Practice of the Learning Organization: Revised & Updated,* (New York: Doubleday, 2006),131.

16 Tom Mullins, "Servant Leaders Celebrate Others," in *Servant Leadership In Action,* ed. Ken Blanchard & Renee Broadwell. (Oakland, CA: Berrett-Koehler Publishers), 77.

17 Shawn Achor, *Big Potential: How Transforming the Pursuit of Success Raises Our Achievement, Happiness, and Well-Being,* (New York: Currency, 2018).

18 AUSA Staff, "Company Command: The Best Advice I've Ever Received," Association of the United States Army, March 10, 2014, https://www.ausa.org/articles/companycommand-best-advice-i've-ever-received.

19 Jamie Johnson, "10 Bill Gates Quotes Every Business Owner Needs to Hear," US Chamber of Commerce, January 7, 2020 https://www.uschamber.com/co/start/strategy/bill-gates-business-quotes.

20 Pamela M. Tripp, *The Culture Cure: Transforming the Modern Healthcare System.* (N.p.: CreateSpace Independent Publishing Platform, 2016).

21 Laura Reid, "'I alone cannot change the world…' - Mother Teresa." *The Skipping Stone* (blog). June 5, 2019. https://www.theskippingstone.com/blogs/news/i-alone-cannot-change-the-world-mother-teresa.

22 Kellerman and Seligman, *Tomorrowmind,* 8-9. Atria Books, New York 2023.

23 Kim Scott, *Just Work: How to Confront Bias, Prejudice and Bullying to Build a Culture of Inclusivity,* (New York: St Martin's Publishing Group, 2021), 95.

24 Scott, *Just Work,* 142.

25 Jim Granat, "Four Benefits of Promoting Talent From Within," Forbes, November 5, 2019, https://www.forbes.com/sites/forbesfinancecouncil/2019/11/05/four-benefits-of-promoting-talent-from-within/.

26 Peter Cappelli, "Your Approach to Hiring is All Wrong," *Harvard Business Review,* May 2019, https://bg.hbr.org/2019/05/your-approach-to-hiring-is-all-wrong#your-approach-to-hiring-is-all-wrong.

27 Simon Sinek Quotes. BrainyQuote.com, BrainyMedia Inc, last modified 2023, https://www.brainyquote.com/quotes/simon_sinek_568162.

28 Jeff Haden, "40 Inspiring Motivational Quotes About Gratitude," *Inc.,* September 12, 2014. https://www.inc.com/jeff-haden/40-inspiring-motivational-quotes-about-gratitude.html.

29 John C. Maxwell, *150 Essential Insights on Leadership*, (Eugene, OR: Harvest House Publisher, 2014), 47.

30 Indeed Editorial Team, "60 Inspirational Quotes for a New Job," Indeed, last modified February 20, 2023, https://www.indeed.com/career-advice/starting-new-job/quote-for-new-job.

31 "Interview," David McCullough, National Endowment for the Humanities, accessed October 3, 2023, https://www.neh.gov/about/awards/jefferson-lecture/david-mccullough-biography.

32 Brian Tracy Quotes. BrainyQuote.com, BrainyMedia Inc, last modified 2023, https://www.brainyquote.com/quotes/brian_tracy_173267.

33 Scott, *Just Work*, 10.

34 Carmine Gallo, "The Maya Angelou Quote That Will Radically Improve Your Business," Forbes, May 31, 2014, https://www.forbes.com/sites/carminegallo/2014/05/31/the-maya-angelou-quote-that-will-radically-improve-your-business/.

35 Jim Harter, "U.S. Employee Engagement Needs a Rebound in 2023," Gallup, January 25, 2023, https://www.gallup.com/workplace/468233/employee-engagement-needs-rebound-2023.aspx.

36 From https://louiscarter.com/32-leadership-coaching-quotes-to-help-you-reach-your-full-potential/ accessed 6/26/23.

37 J.G. Anderson and K. Abrahamson, "Your Health Care May Kill You: Medical Errors," *Studies in health technology and informatics*, 234, (2017):, 13–17.

38 Niki Carver, Vikas Gupta,  and John E. Hipskind,  "Medical Errors," StatPearls, StatPearls Publishing, last modified May 7, 2023, https://www.ncbi.nlm.nih.gov/books/NBK430763/.

39 Haden, "Quotes about Gratitude."

40 Curt Steinhorst, "Didn't You See My Email?," Forbes, January 30, 2023, https://www.forbes.com/sites/curtsteinhorst/2023/01/30/didnt-you-see-my-email/.

41 Ralph Marston Quotes, BrainyQuote.com, BrainyMedia Inc, last modified 2023, **https://www.brainyquote.com/quotes/ralph_marston_132966**.

42 Alok Patel and Stephanie Plowman, "The Increasing Importance of a Best Friend at Work," Gallup, August 17, 2022, https://www.gallup.com/workplace/397058/increasing-importance-best-friend-work.aspx.

43 Lolly Daskal, "24 Empowering Quotes to Start Your Day Right," *Inc.,* July 2, 2015, https://www.inc.com/lolly-daskal/24-empowering-quotes-to-start-your-day-right.html.

44 Carol Bradford, "The Power of Encouragement," Ohio State University College of Medicine, April 2023, https://medicine.osu.edu/ohio-state-medicine-dr-bradford-message/april-2023.

45 Patrick Alain, *The Quick and Easy Performance Appraisal Phrase Book*, Patrick Alain, (Pompton Plains, NJ: Career Press, 2013), 15.

46 Laurie Bassi and Daniel McMurrer, "Maximizing your Return on People," Harvard Business Review, March 2007, https://hbr.org/2007/03/maximizing-your-return-on-people.

47 Bassi and McMurrer, "Maximizing Your Return."

48 James Clear, *Atomic Habits: An Easy & Proven Way to Build Good Habits & Break Bad Ones*, New York: Avery, 2018), 15.

49 Simon Sinek, *The Infinite Game*, (USA: Portfolio/Penguin, 2019).

www.ingramcontent.com/pod-product-compliance
Lightning Source LLC
Chambersburg PA
CBHW030429160726
47991CB00005B/1652